Paynes Prairie

Paynes Prairie
A History of the Great Savanna

Lars Andersen

Pineapple Press, Inc.
Sarasota, Florida

Inquiries should be addressed to:

Pineapple Press, Inc.
P.O. Box 3889
Sarasota, Florida 34230
www.pineapplepress.com

Library of Congress Cataloging in Publication Data

Andersen, Lars, 1956–
    Paynes Prairie : a history of the great savanna / Lars Andersen.— 1st ed.
        p. cm.
    Includes bibliographical references (p.) and index.
    ISBN 1-56164-225-8 (alk. paper)
    1. Paynes Prairie (Fla.)—History. 2. Natural history—Florida—Paynes Prairie. I. Title.

F317.A4 A54 2001
975.9'79—dc21
                                                                00-050210

First Edition
10 9 8 7 6 5 4 3 2 1

Printed in the United States

Illustrations on pages 5, 8, 27, and 49 by Robert Malinowski

Table of Contents ❧

To the memory of my parents,
Dr. Thorkild W. and Lillian Andersen

Acknowledgments

ᘏᕝ

This book has been many years in the making, and in every phase, whether I was exploring the countryside around Paynes Prairie or digging my way through countless documents and historical collections, there were many people who helped. To all of them, I am very grateful. The real credit for this book goes to all of the authors listed in the bibliography. The work of some—such as Amy Bushnell, Dr. Charles Fairbanks, Jerald Milanich, and John Mahon—was very helpful, and these folks deserve special credit.

I'd especially like to thank my brother, Niels, who has not only spent a great deal of time roaming the Prairie with me over the years but has been my companion on many adventures: the elusive Arbuckle Mountain range of Oklahoma, the "woods" of Oregon, the top of Colorado's Continental Divide, and the untamed wilderness of downtown Key West, Florida.

My good friend, Robert Malinowski, who provided the excellent drawings in this book, was also a big help in the field. He, along with his enthusiastic son Daniel, accompanied me on several excursions into the back country around the Prairie and helped with the photographs. The skills of Mark Booth, bush pilot extaordinaire, and his assistant (now wife), Erin Moran, allowed me to take my exploration of Paynes Prairie to the air. Jack McKinney's generosity in allowing me the use of his computer kept this book from being a lifelong project at the helm of an ancient piece of machinery called a typewriter; for that I am truly grateful. Clint Jenkins always believed in me and encouraged me to take chances and reach farther than I would otherwise dare. Lynn Black bravely joined me on many explorations, including a journey through some of the deepest, darkest places imaginable. I will always be grateful.

Others who helped include Sherilyn Reinert and Jim Weimer at Paynes Prairie State Preserve; Larry Johnson, naturalist for the city of Gainesville; and Rusty Studstill. Thanks also to Ben Pickard, Burnham Cooper, and the rest of the staff at the Matheson Historical Center in Gainesville; Leslie Lawhon at the Florida State Archives; the archivists in Special Collections at the P. K. Yonge Library at the University of Florida; and Dan Ronntree and Jude Dawson, for generously sharing their advice and photographic equipment.

I would also like to thank my family and my ex-wife, Virginia, for their patience and support during the years of research and writing that went into this book. I'm especially grateful to Patsy Bass, who fended off those irresistible little distractions like kids and pets and kept things running smoothly at the Adventure Outpost while I slogged through the final stages of editing. Lastly and most, I thank my twelve-year-old son, Niklaus. His boundless curiosity and sense of humor always make our explorations of the Prairie—and every other wild place we find ourselves in—a fantastic adventure. Through his eyes, I am constantly reminded of how amazing the world is and how simple it is to be truly happy.

Introduction

❦

Every day the scene is played out thousands of times. A car speeds through the north Florida countryside along Interstate 75, the driver's gaze mindlessly transfixed on the road ahead. Without any mountains or even a respectable hill to provide visual stimulation, the poor driver struggles to maintain consciousness as an endless panorama of pine and oak forests flashes past his windows.

Suddenly, a few miles south of Gainesville, the forests stop abruptly and the vehicle is launched out onto a vast savanna. His senses aroused, the driver scans the view to one side and then the other. His pulse quickens. But before he has a chance to ponder the wonders around him, the poor fellow is hurled once more into the forest and whisked away by his determined vehicle. Within seconds, his eyes glaze over and his face settles into a mindless grin. He is again at one with the road, never realizing that he has just passed one of the most fascinating places in Florida: Paynes Prairie.

Paynes Prairie has always held a certain fascination for humans, whether it's the bewildered automobile driver at the mercy of his vehicle or the prehistoric Indian standing at the Prairie's edge planning his next meal: mammoth? mastodon? Or should he surprise the family with a twenty-foot-long ground sloth?

For me, it wasn't hunger that brought me to Paynes Prairie but a simple passion for the outdoors. At a very early age, I began romping through the woods along Rattlesnake Creek behind my family's Gainesville home. Like that of all woodland creatures, my range expanded as I grew older, and by my early teens I had "discovered" Paynes Prairie. I began exploring the Prairie every chance I got, often joined by friends and my brother, Niels, whose inspired rendition of "black on yellow, kill a fellow" is believed to have saved an untold number of innocent lives.

Aside from the more serious daytime wanderings, there was also the occasional evening adventure undertaken with the infamous band of rogues known as the Finlians (or FFOs). On those occasions, we would all pile into Henry Shirley's '67 Valiant and head for the Prairie. As Henry skillfully piloted his craft along Wacahoota Road, two or three designated idiots would sit on the hood to watch for snakes and any other nocturnal creatures that might be wandering about.

Nearly fifteen years later, while I was living in Dallas, Texas, Paynes Prairie unexpectedly came back into my life. While researching north Florida's history in preparation for producing an educational audiotape for highway travelers, I was surprised to find that Paynes Prairie played an important role in much of the early settlement and development of north central Florida. Had the Prairie not been here, Florida's history would have been very different. But I was even more surprised to find that there were no books on the subject. By the time I finished producing "The North Florida Adventure" in 1988, my research on the Prairie was well under way. The task was made considerably easier when I moved back to Florida in 1989.

Every year, a growing number of visitors come to explore Paynes Prairie State Preserve. I hope this book will serve to supplement the wealth of information provided by the Preserve staff, the interpretive center, and local museums, and will help make exploration of the Prairie a more enjoyable and fulfilling experience.

Paynes Prairie

1. *Prehistoric Paynes Prairie*

❦

D inosaurs ruled the earth for nearly 160 million years, but none ever laid a foot on Paynes Prairie. The closest any dinosaurs came to the Prairie was the beautiful shoreline that once stretched from present-day Charleston, South Carolina, westward through central Georgia, Alabama, and Mississippi. Any inquisitive dino that paused on that ancient beach to ponder the southern horizon, where Florida resides today, would have seen nothing but an endless expanse of open water. That was during the Cretaceous period, which ended nearly 135 million years ago.

For millions of years, the shells and skeletons of primeval sea creatures settled on the submerged peninsula, layer upon layer, until the accumulated debris was thousands of feet thick. This sediment was then compacted to form the limestone that is Florida's rock foundation. Finally, about twenty-five million years ago, sea levels began to drop worldwide and the Florida landmass surfaced. By then, dinosaurs had long since been extinct.

It is possible that the Florida peninsula temporarily rose above sea level during the early part of the dinosaur's reign, but the layer of rock that would contain any fossil evidence of their presence is thousands of feet below the present land surface, a respectable dig for even the most ambitious dino hunter. To date, the closest areas dinosaur fossils have been found are central Alabama and Mississippi.

The original landscape was somewhat flatter and the climate warmer than it is today. The area now covered by Paynes Prairie was basically flat, void of the basin and sinkholes that we see today. It wasn't until about twenty million years ago that the processes that would eventually form Paynes Prairie began.

These processes, which continue today, begin with rainwater percolating down through the soil surface and interacting with and dissolving the underlying limestone. This creates large pockets underground. Eventually, some of these pockets collapse under the weight of rock and soil, forming a depression on the surface, which we call a sinkhole. Paynes Prairie's huge basin was formed when a number of sinkholes formed close to each other and eventually merged. The bulk of this formation is estimated to have begun about thirty thousand years ago. Around the Prairie, and especially near the northern margin, the rolling hills, numerous sinkholes, caverns, and natural springs are all characteristic of this type of terrain, known as Karst topography.

There's nothing unique about this process. It happens all over Florida. Usually, because the bottom of these depressions is impermeable, they fill with water and form lakes. But what gives Paynes Prairie its unique character is Alachua Sink—a hole in the floor of the basin. Located on the northern edge of the basin, the sink continually drains the water from the Prairie basin, keeping it from becoming a lake. Only during exceptionally heavy periods of rain or when something plugs the sink does Paynes Prairie temporarily become a shallow lake. It is this unique tendency to remain wet while never being allowed to fill that makes Paynes Prairie the ideal habitat for an amazing array of wetland species. But we're jumping ahead.

The newly exposed ground was quickly covered with plant life, and with it came the animals. Florida's earliest plant and animal history is unknown, so researchers must rely on educated guesses when trying to describe the early environment. It wasn't until Florida was about five million years old that events took place near the northern margin of Paynes

Prairie that would give archaeologists their first glimpse of early Florida life. That earliest record of land animals in Florida comes from fossils found while constructing the Interstate 75 overpass at Williston Road (State Road 121).

The site was apparently a small sinkhole into which a number of unwary creatures accidentally fell twenty-five million years ago. Some—such as opossums, bats, squirrels, and an assortment of rodents, snakes, lizards, and box turtles—are still common today. Other victims of the pit, now extinct, were the evolutionary ancestors of some of the animals we know today. *Mesohippus* was a small, three-toed predecessor to the modern horse. There was also *Leptomeryx,* probably one of the earliest forms of deer, as well as a couple of extinct sheep-sized, long-tailed grazers known as oreodonts.

The I-75 site is presumed to have been close to the ancient shoreline and even underwater at times, because along with the remains of land animals are a number of sea creatures such as sharks, stingrays, and bony fish.

Suwannee Straits

At about the same time that the I-75 sinkhole was formed, a wide waterway known as the Suwannee Straits is thought to have divided the Florida peninsula, joining the Atlantic ocean to the Gulf of Mexico. It is possible that the Straits flowed near or over the Paynes Prairie region, which would explain the strange mixture of aquatic and terrestrial animals found at the site.

Early Miocene

The next epoch, the Miocene, began about twenty-four and a half million years ago. Much as it has today, the area had many varieties of reptiles and amphibians, including racers, boas, coral snakes, iguanas, and even Gila monsters. There were even a few token giants such as *Gavialosuchus,* a narrow-snouted crocodilian that reached twenty feet in length; a ten-foot ancestor of today's rattlesnake; and a huge land tortoise called

Geochelone, whose size rivaled that of its present-day relatives on the Galapagos Islands. Birds were also plentiful; many, such as anhingas, ospreys, vultures, kites, hawks, turkeys, and ibises, would be familiar today. Others, such as the flamingo, still survive in various parts of the world but no longer live around Paynes Prairie.

The family of mammals experienced tremendous growth in Florida during the Miocene. This was the high point of the Age of Mammals, and while it's true that dinosaurs hold the endurance record for ruling the earth (a respectable 160 million years), Florida's Miocene mammals are definite contenders for oddness of shapes and behavior. Small predators such as martens and weasels were busy keeping the rodent population in check, while their distant relatives in the dog tribe were after bigger game. Early ancestors of the dog were powerful and often bearlike in appearance.

Also wandering about in the forest were some less-recognizable animal ancestors. Small, dog-sized ancestors of the modern horse browsed alongside the "giant hog," which sometimes reached ten feet in length. There were several varieties of rhinoceros, some with the nasal horn that marks their present-day descendants in Africa, others without. One variety was about the size of a wolf and could run quite fast.

A major event of the Miocene was the evolution of a new type of plant: grass. With the arrival of the grasses, body forms and habits of many animal species changed dramatically. Today, grasses are the favorite ground cover for landscapes worldwide, and we owe the existence of this plant to the early grazers. The constant trampling of hooves gave the plant its ability to endure heavy foot traffic, and by grazing the plants as close to the ground as they could, the animals encouraged the survival of those plants whose growth buds were at or near the soil line. Every time you mow, by imitating the behavior of a prehistoric grazer, you're giving your grass exactly what it wants. Some of the more inconspicuous animals of the early Miocene, such as small humpless camels and deer the size of rabbits, would take advantage of the increasing grasslands to become an important part of the area's fauna later on.

Late Miocene

By the end of the Miocene epoch (about five million years ago), the Paynes Prairie region had developed a very different appearance. Grasslands had become a major feature of the landscape, and temperatures were somewhat cooler. A variety of grazing animals, including several types of horses and antelopes, roamed the open savannas in large herds. There were several breeds of camels, but none had the hump that their modern descendants developed to cope with arid environments. The largest of the camelids preferred to stay close to the forest, where it could take advantage of its long, giraffelike neck to reach foliage twelve feet off the ground.

During the mid-Miocene, the land bridge across the Bering Strait allowed migrations of new kinds of animals to North America and eventually central Florida. Some of the

newcomers were members of the elephant family, sporting a fantastic variety of trunks and tusk arrangements, but none survived the test of time.

In addition to the Bering Strait land bridge that encouraged Asian migrations, another land bridge joined North and South America and allowed a major exchange of species. Among the newcomers from South America were sloths, which would later give rise to a family of behemoths called giant ground sloths, which will be discussed later.

With all of this available game, the predators were also thriving. The dog tribe was represented by several early, hyena-type beasts that were just as content to steal another animal's meal as to go out and kill for themselves. But, without a doubt, the greatest predators of the late Miocene were the cats. The largest was probably *Nimravides*, a true cat that resembled a modern jaguar and weighed nearly 150 pounds. Others, known as sabercats, crossed the Bering land bridge and showed up in north Florida in the mid-Miocene.

One of the most awesome beasts to stalk the central Florida fauna during that or any other time period was the false sabercat. This powerful hunter was not equipped to run for more than short sprints so it had to dispatch its victims quickly. Hiding in ambush, the false sabercat, or *Barbourofelis,* would lunge at its prey, grab it with long retractile claws, then plunge its saberlike teeth into its victim's back. The false sabercat was the ultimate carnivore, with every tooth in its mouth designed for cutting and tearing flesh, a trait seen in no other animal before or since. The best place to see a *Barbourofelis* is a few miles from Paynes Prairie at the Museum of Science and History on the University of Florida campus, where, through the efforts of S. David Webb and his associates, the only complete *Barbourofelis* skeleton in the world resides.

Arrival of Humans

One day about twelve thousand years ago, the wind carried a strange new scent to the animals gathered at Alachua sink. All eyes were focused on the nearby woods, where the smell originated. The underbrush rustled, and out stepped a small pack of strange creatures walking upright on two legs. Man had come to the Prairie.

Those first primitive nomads of the Pleistocene epoch were probably impressed by the animals they saw as they stepped cautiously from the forest. Gathered at the sink, enjoying a midday drink, might have been peccaries, tapirs, and capybaras weighing nearly 150 pounds. The humans may even have seen one of the five-hundred-pound beavers, known as castroides, that lived in the area.

From the high bank above Alachua sink, the tribe of nomads could look along the tree line and perhaps catch a glimpse of the giant ground sloth. This awkward beast was nearly twenty feet long from head to tail, making it the largest animal ever to live in Florida. Its enormous height allowed the giant sloth to browse among leaves high in the trees, where most other animals couldn't reach. Huge claws on its front feet helped the sloth pull leaves into its mouth but also made getting around difficult, forcing it to walk on its knuckles.

Another giant of Ice Age Florida was the glyptodont. It looked very much like its modern descendant, the armadillo, except that it was about ten feet long. Another major difference is that instead of feeding on insects like today's armadillo, the glyptodont preferred to eat grass.

A variety of animals more familiar to us would also have been enjoying the Prairie's tasty selection of grasses and shrubs. Horses had finally evolved into the animal we know today and would have been seen traveling in large herds throughout the region. Camels, llamas, and bison with horns six feet across were also local residents. Mammoths and mastodons, ancestors of the modern elephant, were plentiful. Primitive men had been hunting these large animals for thousands of years and were skilled not only in killing them, but in fashioning tools and clothing from the body parts that weren't eaten. The hunters also knew that where so much game was found, large predators could not be far away. Animals like the dire wolf,

twenty percent larger than today's wolf, lived on the Prairie, as did the more familiar varieties of wolves and coyotes.

Several bear species would also have been wandering the nearby woods. The huge *Tremarctos floridanus* ranged throughout Florida at this time. It was a concern only when angered or cornered since it was probably an herbivore. The Florida panther, today in danger of extinction, was common during the Ice Age, as was the only other cat species found near the Prairie today, the bobcat. Felines that did not survive the pressures of natural selection were the six-hundred-pound saber-toothed cat, or *Smilodon,* and the larger *Felis atrox*, a giant lion that was almost half again the size of modern lions.

By definition, Florida's prehistoric nomads moved on to other parts of the region as dictated by the availability of game and forage. But man now knew about Paynes Prairie and would never again be far away. Within a few thousand years, most of the Pleistocene megafauna was extinct. There are many theories attempting to explain this, including some that point to humans—with their large brains and larger appetites—as part of the cause.

❦

2. *The First People*

The first band of humans arrived at Paynes Prairie nearly twelve thousand years ago, during the late Pleistocene epoch. These newcomers, often referred to as Paleo-Indians, were nomadic hunters and gatherers with a serious appetite for mammoths, mastodons, and the other over-sized beasts that characterized the period. To them, Paynes Prairie was paradise. Thousands of years earlier, their ancestors had crossed the Bering Strait to Alaska and slowly spread their range southward. Like their modern-day descendants, the Paleo-Indians were constantly searching for greener pastures. The quest eventually brought them to Paynes Prairie.

Florida was well suited to the early inhabitants, although it was nothing like today. Much of the world's water was tied up in the vast glaciers of the waning Ice Age, resulting in lower sea levels worldwide. By some estimates, the sea level was nearly thirty-five meters lower than it is today, which would have made Florida nearly twice its present size. Temperatures were cooler and the land was drier, with much more grassland and savanna. The forests were mostly hardwoods, rich in nuts and berries with which the Indians could supplement their diet.

The Paleo-Indians were not hulking, apish brutes but true

"modern humans" of our own subspecies, *Homo sapiens,* with their own spoken language. Like their Asian ancestors, these were short people with black hair and bronze skin. For mutual protection, the Paleo-Indians usually traveled in bands of fifty to one hundred men, women, and children. This also allowed the men to hunt in groups large enough to bring home the occasional mammoth or mastodon. When stalking large beasts, the hunters tried to take advantage of natural geographic or geologic features. For instance, ambushes were laid at river crossings, where an animal could be attacked while wading across. At Paynes Prairie, another tactic might have been to drive animals into the marsh, where they would get mired and could be easily killed.

The large animals of the Ice Age were the driving force of Paleo-Indian life. Where the animals went, so went the tribe. Not only did the Indians obtain most of their food from the animals, but most of their clothing, tools, and weapons were made from the animals' hides and other body parts.

More of these nomadic bands would discover Paynes Prairie in years to come, and, while their lifestyle didn't allow them to settle permanently, they would never forget the bounty they found on the Prairie and would return whenever the game populations were replenished. Over the next five thousand years, Florida's environment slowly changed. By about 7,500 B.C., the weather had become warmer and more damp, allowing oak hardwoods to become the dominant forest type in the area. The Ice Age was ending, and as the retreating glaciers melted, sea levels rose enough to swallow thousands of square miles of the coastal plain, especially along the Gulf.

Archaic Period

With time, the populations of large Pleistocene mammals such as mastodons, mammoths, and giant ground sloths declined, and by 6,500 B.C. the megafauna was gone. These changes forced the people of north Florida to rethink their approach to survival. This transition marks the beginning of the Archaic period. Many new kinds of animals began to show up in the Indian roasting pits around Paynes Prairie. Most had been here all along, but the hunters had chosen to bypass them in favor of the larger animals. Now there was no choice but to eat whatever they could find.

It was during this period that several innovations showed up in the hunters' arsenal. The spear was still their most important weapon, but with the invention of the throwing stick, or atlatl, spears became much more deadly. The spear was laid on top of the atlatl, which was then reared back and swatted over the shoulder, similar to the way a tennis player serves a ball. This hurled the spear with much more force and speed than if it had been thrown by hand. Evidence at some sites in Florida suggest that the Archaic Indians may also have used bolas. These were made by attaching a stone at each end of a long cord. When thrown at a small animal, such as a bird or rabbit, the bola stones would wrap the cord around the animal and disable it.

White-tailed deer were plentiful and became the Indians' favorite prey. To supplement their diet, the people depended more on nuts, berries, and other plant materials than they had before. The Archaic Indians were still semi-nomadic, moving from one area to another to take advantage of seasonal changes in different environments. For example, when shell-fish were plentiful, they would make camp along the coast; when hickory nuts were ripe or hunting was especially good, they would then move to the hardwood forests, such as those around Paynes Prairie.

There seems to have been some sense of religion among the Archaic Floridians. Burials dating from this period included a few simple wooden, stone, and bone artifacts, presumably in anticipation of an afterlife. The corpse itself was given no great reverence. After being partially wrapped in grass, it was lowered into a marsh on a simple platform of branches.

As the people became more settled, they had time to develop new items to make life easier. One such development was pottery. Pottery first appeared in Florida about 2,500 to 2,000 B.C. It's not certain whether Florida Indians learned the process

Prehistoric Boomerangs

Archaeologists have found evidence suggesting the Archaic hunters of Florida used a primitive type of boomerang for hunting. The only problem was that these boomerangs did not return to the thrower. Nonetheless, they were probably very accurate and lethal weapons for hunting small game. The only other place such non-returning boomerangs have ever been found is Australia, where aborigines were eventually able to improve the design to make the returning variety we are familiar with today.

on their own or acquired it from some other region. Either way, it was an important new technology, not only for the Indians, but also for modern-day archaeologists, who categorize certain cultures and time periods by different pottery styles.

By 1,000 B.C., the first meager attempts at cultivation were probably under way around Paynes Prairie. Plants such as gourds and melons were likely the first to be intentionally planted from seed and then tended. Corn, later to become the most important crop to Native Americans, was probably first cultivated on a small scale between 500 and 100 B.C.

As Florida's natives became more settled, the people of each area began to develop their own culture, each with its own individual characteristics. One of the state's first distinctive cultures developed along Florida's Gulf coast and on the Atlantic coastline north of St. Augustine. This is known as the Deptford culture, which began about 500 B.C. and lasted until about A.D. 100 to 200 on the Gulf side, and to about A.D. 600 on the Atlantic coast. It seems that these people didn't have any inland settlements, preferring to live in live oak–magnolia hammocks near coastal marshes and lagoons where they could take advantage of these rich habitats. Some artifacts of the Deptford people have been found near Paynes Prairie, but they were probably left by small bands out hunting or gathering chert, used to make weapons and tools, from nearby limestone outcrops.

The Deptford people were at the southern end of a trade network that stretched far to the north. In exchange for shells and chert, the coastal Indians received many artifacts and ornaments that couldn't be made locally. Copper beads made by tribes in the Great Lakes region were especially prized by the Florida natives.

As contact increased between the Deptfords and their neighbors, cultural and religious ideas and practices were exchanged. The most noticeable addition to Deptford tradition was the practice of burying the dead in mounds. Some archaeologists speculate that the practice began with mounds being built as platforms for the dwellings of important village leaders. At death, the leader's body was laid in the house, which was then burned. Afterward, the charred remains were covered with a layer of dirt. In the Ohio and Mississippi River valleys, some advanced cultures had been building mounds for hundreds of years by the time the practice reached Florida. This was somewhere around 400–300 B.C. However, since the main Deptford settlements were still near the coast, none of the earliest Deptford mounds were built near Paynes Prairie.

The Cades Pond People

About A.D. 100–200, some of the Deptford people moved inland and formed settlements around Paynes Prairie and near the banks of Newnans, Orange, and Lochloosa Lakes. These were the Cades Pond people, named for a site near Santa Fe Lake where one of their burial mounds was first discovered in the 1870s. These were the first year-round residents of this area.

In their own way, the Cades Pond people were almost as dependent on aquatic habitats as their Deptford ancestors, though they were now dealing with fresh water as opposed to salt. About ninety percent of the animals they ate came from lakes and marshes. Some fish were probably caught with hooks or specialized spears called leisters, but the majority were caught with seine nets.

There was probably very little agriculture among the Cades

Pond people, but they easily survived without it. Using the knowledge acquired over thousands of years by their ancestors on forays into this region, the Cades Pond Indians were able to supplement their diet with a wide variety of woodland plants and animals. Just about every kind of animal they could get their hands on was eaten, including an assortment of reptiles and birds as well as skunks, rats, moles, squirrels, rabbits, wolves, black bears, and Florida panthers. But there was no animal as important to the Indians as the deer, whose meat was their main source of protein.

Traps and spears were still the most common means of hunting game, but there may have been a new tool in the Cades Pond hunter's arsenal. Small points, discovered in Cades Pond village sites, may have been used on arrows. If so, this would be the first known use of bows and arrows in the eastern United States.

The practice of building mounds was another feature of the Cades Pond culture that was retained from their Deptford heritage. Many sand mounds that were built by these people can be found in the nearby woods, especially around the eastern margin of Paynes Prairie. The placement of some of these mounds suggests that the Prairie was probably a lake during some or all of the Cades Pond period. There were two kinds of mounds, each with its own special purpose. Large, flat-topped ceremonial mounds, sometimes reaching 150 feet across, were used for temples or charnel houses for the dead. It's difficult for archaeologists to determine exactly how the Cades Pond people used the charnel houses, but some clues can be found in the practices of other southeastern tribes observed by early European chroniclers.

For instance, when an important Choctaw Indian died, his body was wrapped in cloth and set in a small log hut with a number of his prized possessions. The decaying body remained in this state for several months until the time came for interment in a charnel or burial house. Then an old woman picked all of the flesh from the corpse with her fingernails. Referred to as the "vulture woman" in Choctaw society, the old woman always kept her fingernails long for this task. The corpse's flesh was then scattered into the corn fields, and the bones were wrapped in cloth and taken to the charnel house amid much singing and ceremony. There the bundled bones were hung from a pole alongside the many other bundled remains that lined the inside walls.

For the Choctaws, the charnel house was the body's final resting place, but it was a different matter for the people of the Cades Pond culture. After being stored for some time in the charnel house, the bundled remains were either buried in a nearby mound or burned and the ashes buried in the mound or simply scattered on top. Numerous burials were made in the mound until it was essentially full. At that time another mound would be started, or, as was the case with some other southeastern cultures, the entire village may have been abandoned.

Burial mounds are much more numerous than ceremonial mounds in the woods around Paynes Prairie. They vary greatly in size from twenty to eighty feet across and are usually from two to nine feet high with a rounded top. Most of these mounds have been ransacked over the years by misguided treasure hunters. Fortunately, there are some in the vicinity of Paynes Prairie that remain undisturbed.

Alachua-Tradition Cultures

About A.D. 800, a flourishing society in southeastern Georgia mastered the techniques of agriculture, which allowed them more time for other pursuits. As their culture became more advanced, they were able to expand their range southward, eventually displacing the Cades Pond people living near Paynes Prairie. These newcomers were the forefathers of the Timucua Indians who inhabited much of north Florida when Europeans first arrived. The lifestyle of this new culture, known as the Alachua-tradition, was similar to their Cades Pond predecessors in many ways. Hunting and gathering techniques were about the same, as were the foods they ate, except for a greater reliance on corn and the other crops they grew.

Alachua-tradition villages were usually built in oak-hardwood forests, where their favorite wild foods were found. The houses were grouped together, lying twenty to thirty yards apart, with food storage huts and racks for drying meat interspersed among them. Just outside the village were large cultivated fields of corn, squash, and melons. The houses themselves were about twenty feet across, with a framework of upright poles stuck into the ground two or three feet apart. The poles were probably bent toward the center to form a rounded hut. On the outside of this was a layer of palmetto thatch or bark.

Inside near the center of the hut was a pit that contained the cooking fire. Raised benches along the inside wall served as seats by day and beds at night. One problem these early Floridians shared with the people of every other time period, including the present, was bugs. To deal with this problem, the Indians would build a smoky smudge fire under their bed platforms at night, which was probably as uncomfortable for the Indians as it was for the bugs.

Today, village sites and numerous burial mounds, such as this one near Micanopy, remain as silent reminders of the Prairie's ancient past. (Lars Andersen)

The Alachua-tradition people apparently did not make burial mounds. A few mounds are traceable back to the early Alachua-tradition period, but after that, the Indians stopped making them. The new culture thrived in Florida, and it was their descendants, the Timucua, who were here to greet the first white men. By that time, the Timucua had split into many factions, some of which were bitter enemies and would have scoffed at the notion of being related. Those living at Paynes Prairie were called the Potano.

❦

3. The Timucua

When *Europeans first arrived, Timucua Indians lived* throughout Florida north of Tampa Bay and east of the Aucilla River near Tallahassee. There were many factions of the Timucua, each essentially independent. Those living in the vicinity of Paynes Prairie were the Potano, and, while no one is sure, the best guess is that the main village of Potano was near the Prairie's south side. There is very little recorded about the Potano and the Indians living in the area in the 1500s. Spanish explorer Hernando de Soto's army came through in 1539 but stayed only long enough to see there was no gold, then left. There was, however, plenty of contact with other factions of the Timucua, and there is no reason to think that the Potano were any different from their neighbors.

To the northeast, the culture and appearance of Timucuans near present-day St. Augustine were well documented, especially by Jacques Le Moyne, a French artist who accompanied the 1564 French expedition described in a later chapter. Through Le Moyne's eyes, we get our first look at Florida's natives. Outside Le Moyne's drawings, what we know of the appearance and habits of early peoples during their thousands of years in Florida came from lifeless artifacts. With the drawings, suddenly they emerged from the darkness of speculation into the light of documented history.

The Timucua were a tall, well-built people. The women didn't give much attention to their straight black hair, but the men were slaves to fashion when it came to their hairdos. The bulk of their hair was drawn up into a knot on top of the head. This was considered not only attractive but also a handy place for the warriors to stick their arrows for quick access during battle. Below the topknot, a rim of short hairs circled their heads just above their ears.

For jewelry, the Timucua had some copper, gold, and silver ornaments, most of which were obtained through an extensive trade network with other tribes to the north. By the mid-1500s, another source of precious metals developed to the south, where coastal Indians had become the first in a long line of Floridians to enjoy beach-combing for the spoils of wrecked Spanish treasure ships.

Adult males of the tribe usually had tattoos, which they called "scratches," over much of their bodies. Scratches were a sign of rank. When a young brave proved himself in battle, a ceremony was held during which he was engraved with his first tattoo and given a new name. He was then a warrior. In later years, more tattoos were given to the warrior with each great deed, and sometimes he was renamed again. The Timucuan women also wore tattoos. For them, tattoos were a sign of their husbands' achievements and therefore marked their status among the other women.

The process of getting tattooed was said to be extremely painful and would make the recipient ill for several days. The marks were made by pricking the skin with a sharp point, then rubbing cinnebar or lampblack into the fresh wound. A series of these markings would be made into various shapes or designs but never into pictures of people or objects. Occasionally, some underachieving warrior would try to get a tattoo he had not earned. This was forbidden, so the would-be hero was forced to have the marking removed, a process said to be much more painful than the tattooing itself.

There were probably several villages in the Potano district. The main village has not yet been located, but most historians believe it was near the southwestern corner of Paynes Prairie. Le Moyne's description of the Timucuan villages he saw gives us an idea of what a Potano village probably looked like. The chief lived in a large rectangular house in the middle of the village. Around it were a number of circular huts with thatched palm-leaf roofs. These dwellings not only housed the villagers but also served as an insulating barrier between the chief's home and the outside world. As added protection, the entire village was enclosed within a ten- to twelve-foot-tall wall made of stout, wooden poles stuck upright into the ground.

The only way into the village was through a long, narrow passageway formed by a slight overlap in a section of the wall. At each end of the passage stood a small guard hut. The men posted in these huts were said to have had the gift of being able to smell approaching enemy warriors long before seeing them. Outside the village walls were large cultivated fields of corn, squash, pumpkins, and beans. The Timucua had maintained and refined the agricultural heritage passed down to them from their Alachua-tradition ancestors and were managing to harvest two crops per year in Florida's warm climate. The fields were tended by everyone in the village, and at harvest time, each got his fair share. Any surplus was stored in a community storage hut, where it was available to whoever needed it.

The Timucua did a good deal of hunting and gathering to give their diet a little variety. For an extra special treat, they went after alligators. Not only did they enjoy eating the big reptiles, but hunting them gave the warriors a chance to undertake a group hunt reminiscent of the mammoth and mastodon hunts conducted by their ancestors. When a band of hunters found a suitable alligator, they would surround it and, when the animal had its mouth wide open in a threatening gesture, ram a large wooden log down its throat. In this helpless state, the animal was then flipped onto its back and slain with clubs and spears. It wasn't the most glamorous or humane way to get a meal, but it worked. This not only provided food but eliminated

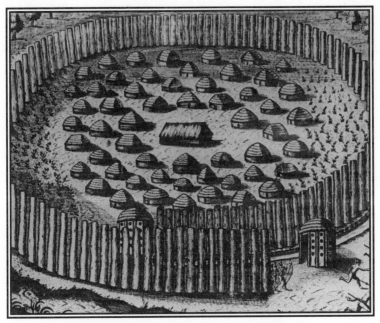

A palisaded Timucuan village showing overlapping walls with a guard hut at each end. (Florida State Archives)

a threat the Timucua took very seriously. For protection against the big reptiles, they would sometimes build small huts at the edge of nearby alligator haunts such as Paynes Prairie or Levy Lake. There, sentinels often kept a lonely watch for the creatures.

Other less exotic species in the Timucuan diet included fish, birds, bear, and deer. The favorite way to prepare meat was to cook it slowly on a rack over a smoky fire. The Indians were masters at getting the most out of everything at their disposal; in the case of the smoking rack, they found it not only did a good job cooking meat, it was also a convenient way to torture criminals or captives from other tribes.

The Timucua had a great knowledge of the plants in their environment, using them not only for food but also for medicines and occasionally for magic potions and spells. Tobacco was extremely important to the Florida Indians. The plant was smoked on special occasions, usually in a long stone or clay pipe. Every aspect of growing and handling the plant was

Jacques Le Moyne's fanciful depiction of Timucua Indians hunting alligators. (Florida State Archives)

taken seriously and carried out under well-defined guidelines. Even setting the fire to create a clearing for the tobacco garden was ritualized and required that the stick used to start the blaze be taken from a tree that had been struck by lightning. As they grew, the plants were carefully tended. When mature, the leaves were individually picked and allowed to cure.

The tobacco plant was thought to have magical powers. If an Indian decided to use some of his tobacco for magic, he took it to the village medicine man. Then, at a special place and time, the medicine man took the bundle and "remade" it, twisting it around in his hands and spitting into it. There were several ways of handling the tobacco to allow the magic to work. One method was to place some of the herb on a spot where the intended victim would be sure to step or sit on it. Another strategy was to blow smoke from the plant into an area where the targeted person would soon pass. One sort of mischief that a Timucuan man was capable of with his "remade" tobacco was making a woman fall in love with him. This could be achieved

Origin of the Barbecue

The Indian smoking rack was adopted by early French explorers who called it a *boucan*. In later years, French settlers who hunted hogs in the backwoods of Haiti and used the racks to smoke their meat became known as *boucaneers*. When French pirates began to terrorize Florida and the Caribbean area, they inherited the nickname of their hog-hunting brethren, changing the spelling slightly to buccaneer. The Spanish, on the other hand, called the grill a *barbacoa*, and it was this term that eventually evolved into today's barbecue.

by blowing the smoke directly onto his intended victim.

In addition to its uses for love and leisure, the Timucua also made some medicines from the tobacco plant. Mixed with an infusion of red sumac and then dried, the herb, when smoked, was thought to cure ailments of the head and chest. To purify the body, the Timucua would smoke tobacco until they vomited, an act that many tribes felt to be extremely invigorating. The quest for nausea was carried even further with cassine, or "black drink," made from yaupon holly. The plant's scientific name, *Ilex vomitoria*, attests to the quality that endeared it to native tribes wherever it was found, both in North and South America. To prepare the black drink, yaupon leaves were first parched over a fire and then hot water was poured over them into a pot. This was then ceremoniously boiled and stirred for several hours. In some southeastern tribes, women were not allowed to talk or even move when the brewing vessel's lid was lifted, as this was thought to impart some evil spirit into the concoction. If such an unfortunate contamination happened, the entire batch was thrown out and the offending squaw beaten. The Timucua were less stringent, allowing women to help prepare the drink. But neither they nor young boys of the village were allowed to drink it.

The active drug in yaupon is similar to caffeine. The drink was tried and liked by Europeans when they arrived and was used into the 1800s in some parts of the Carolinas. Some reports even went so far as to call it addictive. Besides its emetic qualities already mentioned, the black drink was used to relieve many ailments. But it was the warriors who were most fond of it. For days before going into battle, they would fast, drinking only the black drink. They said it strengthened their stomachs and gave them strength and agility in battle. When entering battle, the Indians carried only their weapons and a gourd full of black drink.

Making war was an important part of Timucuan life. The Timucuans engaged in ritual warfare between neighboring villages. The winner of a battle was determined not by who killed the most people, but by who made the first kill. Their arsenal included clubs, spears, and bows and arrows. One favorite tactic used by the warriors was to sharpen their fingernails before battle so they could slash their enemies. The skilled fighter would try to gash his opponent's forehead in hopes of blinding him with his own blood. After the war, arms and legs of fallen enemy warriors were sometimes cut off and taken home, where they were hung on poles around the central plaza as part of the victory celebration.

Death was another occasion for ritual. On top of a warrior's grave, his loved ones placed his favorite black drink vessel, usually a shell. The warrior's wife then went into mourning, cutting her hair very short. She could not remarry until it had grown to her shoulders. A chief's grave was covered with a sand hill, which was much smaller than the burial mounds of earlier tribes. After the burial, the entire village went into mourning, abstaining from food and drink and shaving their heads. After three days, village life resumed, but for the next six months, a select group of women stopped whatever they were doing at three specific times each day and broke into an eerie death wail.

So it was that many generations of Timucua Indians were born, lived their lives, and died in the village of Potano near Paynes Prairie. Life was never easy, but they had achieved equilibrium with their environment and neighboring tribes. Then, one day in 1539, a messenger from the villages to the south brought news of a boatload of strange, bearded white men having come ashore. With this news, the final, tragic chapter of their tribe's existence had begun.

4. De Soto and the Conquistadors

✿

T he summer of 1539 started out like any other for the Timucua Indians of Paynes Prairie. By midsummer, however, runners from tribes to the south were bringing tales of strange invaders from faraway lands—metal-skinned giants riding four-legged beasts and armed with thundering sticks capable of killing from a great distance.

Three months earlier, an army of Spanish soldiers led by the conquistador Hernando de Soto had landed at Charlotte Harbor, south of Tampa. De Soto was a seasoned warrior whose role in the plundering of Peru's Inca empire had brought him wealth and helped him secure the title of *adelanto*, or governor, of Florida. Inspired by the treasures taken by conquistadors in other parts of the New World, de Soto's first official act in Florida was to explore and ransack his new domain.

After some preparation, de Soto and 620 soldiers left Charlotte Harbor and headed northward through the peninsula. With them they had 223 horses, a number of mules and cows, six packs of bloodhounds, and thirteen hogs. De Soto's methods of exploring were typical for that time period—eat the natives' food, tell them you mean no harm, then take several of their strongest youngsters as slaves and guides. Sometimes the

Spaniards would even go so far as to take the village chief hostage to ensure safe passage. One favorite method of "encouraging" the Indians to cooperate and gain their unwavering loyalty was to threaten to throw them into a pack of underfed bloodhounds.

The soldiers relied heavily on the Indians for food, devouring everything they could, including the villagers' pet dogs, which the soldiers took great pride in shooting on sight. Although skilled in the art of warfare, the conquistadors' hunting abilities did not much exceed stalking pets.

Indian runners kept the villagers abreast of the Spanish army's approach, but it's doubtful any of them really knew what to expect. On August 12, 1539, the Spaniards paraded into Potano. Armor-clad, bearded, and mounted on horses (which the Indians had never seen), the Europeans were unlike anything the Potano could have imagined. The record of what transpired between de Soto's men and the Indians of Paynes Prairie is vague. In fact, the only firsthand account, that of the Gentleman of Elvas, simply states that the soldiers spent the night at Potano. We can only draw from what we know about conquistador behavior and assume that when the Spaniards rode away from the village, they had some new Indian slaves on whose backs rode a considerable amount of the Potano food supply.

Hernando de Soto. (Florida State Archives)

There is more written about what happened in the days following the Spaniards' stop at Paynes Prairie. Garcilaso de la Vega, the son of a conquistador in Peru, used to listen to the tales told by his father's comrades when they came to visit. In his later years he became a writer, often relying heavily on those firsthand accounts. In *Florida of the Inca*, in a description of de Soto's expedition, Garcilaso describes de Soto's dealings with a village called Ochile. There has been some speculation that this village was just north of Paynes Prairie, but the record is far too vague. Nonetheless, Garcilaso's account of the events at Ochile is an interesting example of how de Soto and other explorers of that time dealt with America's natives.

Upon their arrival at Ochile, de Soto's troops immediately stormed their way to the village center and surrounded the chief's large house. Chief Ochile, his guards, and a number of villagers who had sought refuge in the building refused to come out. De Soto was faced with a language barrier but, through interpreters, was soon able to inform the chief that he would burn him alive if he did not surrender. With this, the chief promptly came out of the house, enthusiastically welcoming his new friend to Ochile.

De Soto and his conquistadors. (Florida State Archives)

That night, de Soto returned to his previous campsite, stating that he was concerned about the numerous small hamlets, each with three to six buildings, that he had seen scattered across a beautiful valley near Ochile. If Ochile were in fact in this area, de Soto's "valley" could have been Paynes Prairie, but again we can't be sure. The next day, de Soto returned to Ochile. He learned that Chief Ochile was one of three brothers, each a chief of his own village. The oldest was Vitachuco, head chief of the whole region, whose large village lay many miles to the north. Vitachuco's village bore his name, in keeping with an apparent tradition among the Timucua to name their villages after the chief.

For several days, de Soto sent word to Vitachuco that he wanted to talk. At first the great chief did not respond. Then he started sending two or three messengers a day. Each time, the runners would herald their arrival by sounding a bugle, then, after jogging into the village center, would proceed to list for de Soto an impressive assortment of curses and spells that had been cast his way. Being swallowed by the earth, having trees dropped on them, and being assaulted by venomous birds were among the ugly fates that Vitachuco had in store for the Spaniards if they should head toward his village.

At last, Vitachuco agreed to receive the army of conquistadors but secretly intended to ambush and slay them. De Soto's interpreter, Juan Ortiz, learned of the plot and warned his leader. At Vitachuco, de Soto led his men toward the intended ambush, but before the trap was sprung, the Spaniards attacked. Three hundred Timucuans were killed. Many of the others, including Chief Vitachuco, were taken hostage. As they sat in confinement, the captives plotted an escape. Their opportunity came later as Vitachuco was being questioned by de Soto. At a moment when his captors let down their guard, the chief gave a signal, and each of his warriors lunged at the nearest Spaniard. At the same moment, the chief swung around and smashed de Soto in the face, knocking out several teeth. By the time de Soto regained consciousness, Vitachuco lay cold on the ground with a dozen sword wounds in him.

De Soto now had a new problem. In keeping with common practice among Spanish conquistadors throughout the New World, de Soto had been leading the Indians to believe he was a god. This made getting knocked out hard to explain. Rather than try, he ordered that all Indians who had seen the incident be executed. The remainder were taken as slaves.

The conquistadors headed north after the massacre at Vitachuco. In a few short weeks, the Spanish soldiers had destroyed a large part of north Florida's native population and left the survivors without enough food to endure the winter. De Soto would spend the next couple of years searching throughout the Southeast for gold that wasn't there. Finally, the Indians of Louisiana ended his fruitless quest. He had still been claiming that he was a god, so when he died his soldiers had to secretly toss his corpse into the Mississippi River.

There is no further mention of Ochile in later accounts.

Potano, on the other hand, is mentioned in documents for the next century and appears to have become a powerful tribe by the 1560s.

Hinestrosa: First White Woman in Florida

The first white woman to come through the Paynes Prairie region was a stowaway among de Soto's troops during the 1539 expedition. Heartsick at the thought of being apart from her conquistador husband, Francesca Hinestrosa disguised herself as a soldier and joined the expedition. Decked out in the standard armored vest and helmet of a soldier, Hinestrosa clanked and clattered through the Florida wilderness alongside her husband and the other conquistadors. For a while she was successful at keeping her identity hidden, but before long de Soto learned the secret of this baby-faced "soldier."

The army was too far along to send her back, so she was kept on to cook and help tend to the sick and wounded. Freed from having to suppress her femininity, she could now indulge herself in whatever finery she could find in the Florida wilderness. As the expedition moved from village to village, Hinestrosa's collection of trinkets and native jewelry grew. Most cherished was her collection of pearls. Even though they were low-quality oyster pearls, damaged by the Indian practice of roasting the shells to get them open, to her they were priceless.

For almost two years, Hinestrosa waded through every swamp and faced every hardship that befell the expedition. By now she had proven herself to be a valuable member of the party. Perhaps more than anyone, her husband, Hernando Bautista, was glad she had come along, and by the spring of 1541 she was pregnant. The seed had been planted that would have borne the first European child in North America, but fate would have it otherwise. In March 1541, while camped among Chickasaw Indians in Mississippi, the Spaniards came under attack from their discontented Indian hosts. A flaming arrow struck the hut in which Hinestrosa was staying. She managed to escape but, remembering her pearls, ran back into the burning hut. The structure collapsed, killing her and her unborn child.

❦

5. *European Invaders*
❧

There were many things about de Soto's soldiers that had amazed the Potano, but their greed wasn't one of them. The Potano had been the victims of greed before, and while they had never seen "gold fever," they recognized the symptoms. Throughout the period of Indian occupation, Paynes Prairie was known for its wealth of chert, an impure form of flint. This smooth, hard stone can be easily worked into many kinds of tools and can be given a razor-sharp edge, making it highly prized for making spear points and arrowheads. With their monopoly of north Florida's best chert outcroppings, located around the Prairie and throughout the western half of today's Alachua County, the Potano had considerable power. Unfortunately, it also made them the target of many conquest attempts by nearby tribes.

One of their most bothersome neighbors was another tribe of Timucua, the Outina, who lived to the east near the St. Johns River. In the 1560s, the Outina allied themselves with European forces attempting to settle on the east coast. They were quick to take advantage of having these powerful allies, convincing an army of French soldiers and later a Spanish force to join them in a series of raids into Potano.

Following de Soto's unwelcome intrusion, the Potanos enjoyed a quarter century unaware of the mounting European presence in the outside world. By showing that Florida was relatively void of riches, de Soto had dulled Spain's interest in her Florida lands and allowed the Indians on Paynes Prairie to resume their normal lifestyle. But in 1564, two ships entered the St. Johns River and deposited an army of French soldiers onto the sands of Florida. In those early days of discovery and exploration, there was a lot of confusion and conflict over claims to land, and the French were now challenging Spain's hold on Florida. In a transparent attempt to give their claim some validity, the newcomers named the land "New France."

Under the leadership of René Laudonnière, the soldiers went to work building a fort, which they named Caroline after their fourteen-year-old king, Charles IX. After completing Fort Caroline on the river's south bank just east of today's Jacksonville, Laudonnière turned his attention to seeking gold. It was this pursuit that would eventually bring the Frenchmen to Paynes Prairie. When asked about gold, the local Indians told enticing tales of the "Apalatchy" (Appalachian) Mountains, six days' travel to the northwest, where rich deposits of gold and silver were located. Laudonnière was not too concerned about the distance but knew that there would be many villagers along the way with whom he would have to bargain for passage.

In his journal, Laudonnière noted, "The Spaniards in their conquests always entered into alliances, pitting one king against the other." It was toward that end that he began allying himself with many local tribes, giving special attention to the powerful Chief Outina, whose domain separated the French settlement from the beckoning western frontier. This alliance would serve both sides well. In exchange for getting safe passage and assistance in reaching the gold mines of Apalatchy, the French soldiers would help Outina destroy their hated Potano rivals.

In August 1564, nearly three months after arriving in Florida, Laudonnière sent his ensign, Lord d'Arlac, to live with Outina, "hoping that the good will of that great chief would greatly help me in my future discoveries." Outina wasted little time in testing the new alliance. The first attack came in mid-September. D'Arlac and six French soldiers accompanied two hundred of Outina's warriors into the Paynes Prairie region. After traveling all night, they stormed the village of Potano at daybreak.

The Potano were taken completely by surprise, not only by the attack, but also by the musket fire that erupted from the ranks of the invaders. Lord d'Arlac chose his marks carefully and, with one of his first shots, killed the village chief. This threw the Potanos into an even greater panic, and they ran for the woods. Many were killed, and a number of men, women, and children were taken as prisoners. The French lost one soldier in the battle but had made a believer of Outina. The raid was a victory for Outina but had hardly affected the strength of the Potano tribe. By the following spring, Outina was eager to again unleash his new French allies on his hated neighbors. He sent a request to Laudonnière at Fort Caroline for twelve to fifteen armed soldiers. To his delight, he received thirty.

After two days of preparation, the army began their westward march. The French soldiers, commanded by Lieutenant d'Ottigni, were put in the lead. Behind them came three hundred of Outina's warriors. Food and supplies were "carried by women, young boys, and hermaphrodites," which Laudonnière claimed was customary. (Among North American Indians, transvestites and male homosexuals were often used for such tasks and were referred to as *berdaches*.)

About eight miles from Potano, a scouting party spied three Potano Indians fishing from a canoe in a lake. They rushed the fishermen, hoping to prevent any from escaping to alert the village. Two did escape, and the third was shot by arrows, then had both arms and his scalp removed for war trophies. This grizzly practice is documented in several accounts of Timucuan customs and depicted in gruesome detail by the artist Jacques Le Moyne, who was at Fort Caroline during this period. Outina feared that, having been warned, the Potano would be waiting for them. The tribal *jarua*, or medicine man, wasn't much of a comfort to the nervous Outina. After performing the prescribed contortions and ritual chanting, he informed his chief that two thousand Potano were waiting for him. Outina decided to go home.

Upon learning of Outina's desire to retreat, Lord d'Ottigni became enraged, proclaiming that he and his thirty soldiers would attack by themselves if necessary. Outina was not prepared to live with such shame, so he reluctantly ordered his warriors to invade. To d'Ottigni's amazement, the Potano were found exactly where the shaman said they would be—and in the same numbers. For three hours, the battleground was a chaos of war cries and gun blasts. Many Potano warriors were killed, but most escaped into the hardwood forests. Once again, d'Ottigni strongly urged Outina to pursue the enemy, this time with no success. To the Indians, this had been a bloodbath, and they were quite content to call it a victory.

French soldiers never again bothered the Indians of the Paynes Prairie region. By the end of that year, most of the soldiers who had so mercilessly killed the people of Potano were

This picture, copied by Theodore De Bry from a drawing by Le Moyne, shows the Outina and their French allies attacking Potano. Could this open savanna be the first drawing of Paynes Prairie, which was in the heart of Potano country? (Florida State Archives)

themselves massacred by a force of Spaniards led by Pedro Menéndez de Avilés. The province of New France had barely had time to find its way onto any maps before it was gone. Among those who escaped the slaughter were Laudonnière and Jacques Le Moyne, whose pictures, while somewhat exaggerated and stylized, represent the earliest and most in-depth studies of American Indian life in its natural state.

The removal of the French from Florida did not end the Potanos' problems. Following their victory, the Spanish wasted no time in securing their reclaimed Florida holdings. The settlement of St. Augustine was fortified, and, as the French had done, the Spanish attempted to befriend the local Indian tribes. For two years, Menéndez tried to remain neutral in the intertribal politics in the St. Augustine area. But by the summer of 1567, the Spanish found themselves reluctantly allied with Outina and, like the French before them, were soon called upon to prove their sincerity. The target, once again, was Potano.

An army of eighty Spanish soldiers was sent out from St. Augustine in August 1567. Under the leadership of Captain Pedro de Andrada, the column made its way along the old Indian trail toward Paynes Prairie. This time, the Potano were ready. As the soldiers passed through a thick, hardwood hammock, the woods suddenly erupted in a cacophony of Indian war cries and a shower of arrows. The skirmish was brief. When it was over, many of the Spaniards lay dead, including Andrada. Once again, the powerful Potano had held off European invaders, an almost unheard-of feat in the early days of conquest. Soon, however, another wave of Europeans would make their way into Potano country. This time, instead of swords and lances, they carried Bibles and disease, and the results would be tragic.

❦

6. *Rancho de la Chua*
🎵

A*fter wiping out the French settlement at Fort Caroline,*
the Spaniards, under Pedro Menéndez, began the second part of their mission—making a settlement of their
own. France's attempt to settle in Florida had shown the
Spanish how badly they needed to protect their claim. Every
year, galleons loaded with the plundered treasures of the Aztec
and Inca empires made their way along Florida's east coast on
the journey to Spain. To leave this strategic coastline unpro-
tected would be inviting disaster.

The Spaniards wasted no time. In fact, as the last
Frenchmen were systematically slaughtered on the dunes at
Matanzas Inlet, construction was well under way on a tiny settlement ten miles to the north. This was St. Augustine, the first
permanent settlement of Europeans in North America. For the
next two centuries, the culture, religion, and diseases of the
outside world would be funneled through this small town into
the Florida interior, eventually resulting in the extermination of
Florida's entire native population.

The Potano at Paynes Prairie were aware of the new St.
Augustine settlement but, aside from Andrada's attack, had little contact with the newcomers. The Spaniards were there

only to protect their holdings and wanted as little to do with the Florida interior as possible. Only the Indians living near St. Augustine had to deal with the white men, whose ignorance about farming made them almost completely dependent on the Indians' supplies for sustenance.

The Spanish government at St. Augustine "gave" the Timucua title to all lands within a nine-mile radius around their own villages and "old fields." The Spanish felt that they were being extremely generous to the natives, and, compared to previous dealings, they were. Still, the Timucua felt cheated. They had no concept of "owning" land, and besides, who did these newcomers think they were, telling them where they could and could not live? Hard feelings developed between the two sides, which lasted many years. Occasionally, some adventurous Spaniard would plant an orchard or set his cattle to graze in the Potano region. The Indians, in an effort to convey their feelings about the matter, would occasionally set fire to the crops and kill the cattle.

The Christian Missions

Another faction of the Spanish colonists who had an eye on Florida's hinterlands were Christian monks. Here, as in other parts of the world, the monks felt compelled to eliminate the natives' religion and replace it with Christianity. To this end, the determined priests would make frequent trips into the heart of Potano country, preaching to and converting as many Indians as possible. On these occasions, the natives would gather around and watch curiously as the robed priests chanted, gestured, and sang their way through their impassioned lectures on Christianity. The presentations were often effective, prompting some of the Indians to abandon their old beliefs in favor of the white man's religion. An additional number were probably swayed to at least act interested when they saw the tools and trinkets handed out and traded away by the missionaries. Years of experience had taught the monks that there was more than one way to win converts.

The incredible array of implements and tools brought by

the newcomers made quite an impression on the Indians. At first they were a novelty. Then, as the Potano got more used to them, the implements became a necessity. Whether they liked it or not, the Potanos' lifestyle was becoming dependent on things they could get only from the Europeans. It was an uneasy alliance that was maintained more out of mutual necessity than affection.

In 1600, the Potano and the Spanish at St. Augustine called an end to the hostilities that had marred their relationship for many years. The Indians offered to supply labor and food to the garrison at St. Augustine. With the Timucuans' approval, a chain of missions was set up across north Florida. They were built on or near the two main roads that connected St. Augustine to the Apalachee district around present-day Tallahassee.

The closest mission to Paynes Prairie was San Francisco de Potano, just north of today's Gainesville. This mission, like the others, served not only as a meeting place for worship, but as a minor trading post. The Indians living near Paynes Prairie frequently made the journey to San Francisco to trade their wares.

The Mission San Francisco

The Mission San Francisco de Potano was built near Fox Pond in the San Felasco Hammock north of Gainesville. It is believed that the name San Felasco was derived from San Francisco. In order to maintain a presence among the Potano, who were converting in growing numbers, a small outpost, or *vista,* as it was called, was set up south of the Prairie near Orange Lake. Apalo was its name, and, while it wasn't continually occupied, it was visited regularly by a priest, who would hold services for the Indians. As with all such stations, Apalo was located at the edge of one of the Indian villages.

The new religion and the introduction of the trappings of civilization destroyed the Timucuans' traditional lifestyle. As the Indians became increasingly accustomed to the white man's ways and dependent on his trade, they started moving closer to the missions. This proved fatal for many since they still had no resistance to the white man's diseases. With the ever-increasing contact, more epidemics were inevitable. The early 1600s were marked by several plagues. The years between 1613 and 1617 were especially bad, leaving nearly half of the Timucua population dead. Years later, from 1649–1659, measles, smallpox, and typhus epidemics further decimated Florida's native population. Those Potano who kept their distance from the missions fared better than those who moved close, but even they were affected by the numerous plagues that swept through the region.

Meanwhile, back in Europe, the Spanish government was eager to have the Florida colony become more self-sufficient. Much of the Spanish Floridians' food had to be imported since there was very little farming or ranching going on. Any large-scale operation would have to depend heavily on the native population for labor and land. The Spanish authorities in St. Augustine tried to buy land from the Potano on which to raise cattle. The Indians, having no real concept of land ownership, were uncooperative. Frustrated in their attempts to deal with the Indians, the Spaniards started parceling out land anyway.

A Spanish mission in Florida. (Florida State Archives)

La Chua Ranch

By the 1640s, conditions were right for large-scale cattle ranching in the Florida interior, and the Paynes Prairie region was ideal. The Indian population was so small that ranchers would not have to worry about being attacked. On the other hand, there were still enough Potano to supply cheap labor. The Prairie's location was also perfect. The land was the most fertile in all of Florida, and its central location made it an unlikely target for pirates—or so everyone thought.

Francisco Menéndez Marqués, a descendent of St. Augustine founder Pedro Menéndez de Avilés, started a cattle ranch in the Potano region late in the 1640s. He had barely gotten the operation under way when he died in St. Augustine during the yellow fever plague of 1649. His family continued to operate the ranch for many years from its base at St. Augustine, the Potano providing most of the labor.

In 1656, with the English trying to establish footholds along the east coast and in the Caribbean, Spanish authorities at St. Augustine pressured the Potano and other Timucua tribes to supply more manpower. The Indians' frustration with their Spanish neighbors deepened. Finally, in 1656, when some of the Indians were made to carry their own rations of corn on their backs to St. Augustine, they decided they had been pushed far enough and revolted.

The "Great Rebellion" lasted for about eight months. Interestingly, most of the fighting took place between the rebellious Indians and those loyal to the Spanish. Anything even remotely connected to the Spanish presence was destroyed. This included the cattle of Don Francisco Menéndez Marqués' ranch, which were killed and left where they died. Cows that managed to escape the marauding Indians roamed freely around the countryside, surviving quite well without the help of human keepers. On paper, the land remained in the Menéndez Marqués name, but in reality the Potano were once again in full control of their ancestral homelands.

In 1668, St. Augustine was raided by a band of pirates led by Robert Searles. Sixty people were killed and the town pillaged. The authorities in Havana now realized how vulnerable their important garrison at St. Augustine really was. Preparations were made to build what would be the strongest fortress in Spanish Florida. Supplies and manpower were sent from all parts of New Spain, and the recruitment of laborers from Timucua villages was stepped up.

With the population and economy booming, the time seemed right for reviving the inland cattle industry, or so the Menéndez Marqués family thought. Around 1670, Francisco's son, Thomás Menéndez Marqués, the royal accountant in St. Augustine, resigned his position and moved to Paynes Prairie. There he took the remnants of his father's old operation and turned it into the largest cattle ranch in Spanish Florida. He named his domain *La Chua*, a Potano word meaning "jug," which the Indians used when referring to Alachua Sink on the north edge of Paynes Prairie. On the high ground near Alachua Sink, Don Thomás built a large hacienda close to the old Spanish road. From there he controlled hundreds of square miles, mostly to the north and west, upon which his cattle were allowed to roam untended and unfenced.

During the winter months, Don Thomás' herds would spend most of their time in the forests, grazing the lush vegetation that was and still is found there throughout the year. Each spring they would return to the open prairie to graze on the tender new grass. Here they were rounded up, counted, and branded. Some of them were then driven to St. Augustine to be slaughtered. Those cattle that Don Thomás sent to St. Augustine went only because the government required it. Had it been up to him, he would have sent them all to Cuba by way of the San Martin River, the Spaniards' name for the Suwannee–Santa Fe River system. Not only did he get paid more for his ranch products there, the distance to the San Martin was about half of that to the east coast.

On the San Martin, a small outpost had been built during a period of unrest around 1611. Located about twelve miles upstream from the mouth near the present Old Town Hammock, this was the first fortified stronghold in the Florida interior. In later years the Franciscans built the Mission San Martin nearby, where the lower Spanish road crossed the river. Coming by way of the lower road, Don Thomás' ranch hands would load the goods onto launches that frequently made the journey up river to the San Martin outpost. The Spanish government was aware of this outlet but made only feeble attempts to collect duties there.

The Legacy of Don Thomás Menéndez Marqués

In Taylor County, along the Fenholloway River, historians believe Don Thomás Menéndez Marqués, owner of La Chua Ranch, built what was long known as "Thomas' Old Mill" near present Moseley Hall. Thomas Mill Hammock, Thomas Mill Island, Thomas Run, Thomas Mill Shoals, and an ancient route known as Thomas Mill Road are all thought to have been named for this mill.

Thomás was a clever businessman. In Havana, he traded his ranch products for rum, which was then taken directly to the St. Marks River and traded for furs from the Apalachee region. Business went well for Don Thomás, so well, in fact, that it came to the attention of a band of French pirates based on Anclote Key near Tampa Bay. In June 1682, thirty-five of them sailed up the San Martin River, then, guided by a captured river pilot, made their way over land to Paynes Prairie. In the middle of the night, when everyone was asleep, the cutthroats attacked La Chua's headquarters. Don Thomás was captured along with his son-in-law and four servants. The pirates said that the hostages would be set free only when they were given 150 cows and a sack of money. Having made their demands, the pirates torched the buildings and headed for the San Martin with their captives. On the way, a band of Potano ambushed the outlaws and set Don Thomás and the others free.

Two years later, another band of buccaneers, apparently having a bad year on the high seas, made their way to Don Thomás' rebuilt hacienda. This group came north from the Withlacoochee River. Luckily for Don Thomás, these rogues were even less successful than their predecessors, finding no one at the hacienda and nothing of great value to steal.

In 1684, Don Thomás inherited the position of royal accountant in St. Augustine. With falling beef prices and the attention he had to give his new job, Don Thomás' interest in the ranch waned. The garrison at St. Augustine depended on supplies from La Chua, so the authorities were forced to take control of the operation. As the years passed, people found the free-ranging black cattle of La Chua too much to resist. Runaway slaves and hungry Indians enjoyed the "minimum effort, maximum return" of hunting tame cows. People caught herding these cows were punished by having their ears cut off.

In 1704, after a failed attempt to take St. Augustine, Col. James Moore led fifty English colonists from South Carolina and a thousand Creek warriors on an invasion of north Florida. Making their way along the old Spanish road, the raiders burned down all missions and anything else that hinted of Spanish influence. The Apalachee and Timucua peoples were killed by the hundreds. Many others were captured and sold into slavery.

On September 3, 1704, Creek Indians attacked La Chua Ranch and the blockhouse that had been built for defense. One of the ranch hands was killed and four others captured. La Chua Ranch lay silent, except for the ever-present black cows that continued their humble existence in blissful ignorance of the drama being played out around them. The Spanish governor at St. Augustine, however, was not ready to give up on this important area just yet. A small detachment of soldiers was posted at the fortified blockhouse on Don Thomás' abandoned compound. Working in armed bands, the soldiers were able to maintain a sporadic flow of meat and ranch products to the newly completed Castillo de San Marcos.

The Creek warriors also had not completely abandoned the area. For several years after Moore's invasion, the Creeks continued, with aid from their English allies, to attack the Indians of the Apalachee and Timucua regions. As the Creek raiding parties continued to carry off slaves and cattle, the Indians of north Florida were fast approaching extinction.

Don Patricio's Last Stand

The Apalachee Indians were the hardest hit during Moore's initial campaign. By the time he was through with their homeland in the Panhandle, only several hundred Apalachees had managed to escape to other areas. One band from the village of Ivitachuca came to Paynes Prairie. Led by Chief Patricio Hinachuba, the refugees moved to a place called Abosaya near the La Chua headquarters. With Spanish soldiers residing at Paynes Prairie and another contingent posted at the Mission San Francisco de Potano to the north, Patricio felt this would be a safe haven.

In a matter of weeks, the Apalachees built a stockaded village, which they named Ivitachuco. The structure had been complete for just a few days when a Creek war party invaded the La Chua Ranch and the surrounding area. Two missions near San Francisco were sacked as the warriors made their way south toward La Chua. But upon reaching the ranch, they found the garrisoned blockhouse to be more than they wanted to deal with. The soldiers watched nervously from the stronghold until, at last, the warriors turned and headed home, no doubt with a number of La Chua cattle in tow.

Throughout the winter of 1704-05 the raids continued. Then, in late spring 1705, the governor sent a troop of soldiers to La Chua on information that a large attack was being planned by the Creeks. Patricio went to St. Augustine for more supplies; while he was gone, two hundred Creeks attacked Ivitachuco. The governor immediately mustered a troop of one hundred soldiers to ride with Patricio back to the village. Along the way, the soldiers encountered a large number of Creek warriors, and a skirmish ensued. Patricio, concerned for his people, rode on with his own men. When he reached La Chua, Patricio found the countryside swarming with Creek warriors. For several days the chief was unable to get to Ivitachuco. When he did, he found his people starving and destitute.

Continued pressure from the marauding Creeks made life miserable for everyone around La Chua. In January 1706, four Apalachees were attacked by three Timucuans as they were hunting cattle. Three were killed and the other escaped. True to Apalachee custom, the one surviving warrior set out to avenge the death of his companions. Two of the Timucuans involved left the area; the third sought sanctuary in the mission at San Francisco. Patricio reluctantly decided that the only safe place for his people would be near St. Augustine. The village of Ivitachuco was abandoned and the Apalachees moved to a village just south of the Castillo de San Marcos. Any feeling of security that Patricio may have felt was short lived. The Creeks were determined to rid the earth of their Apalachee and Timucua rivals. A couple of months after their arrival, Patricio's village was attacked. Many of the Apalachees were killed, including Patricio.

Back at La Chua, the soldiers were also uneasy with their situation. They spent more energy trying to stay alive than tending cattle. On April 30, 1706, on orders from Governor Martinez, the soldiers burned the blockhouse and returned to St. Augustine, thus ending the Spanish cattle empire of La Chua.

7. *The Seminoles*

With the Spaniards gone from La Chua, north central Florida belonged once again to the Indians. Creek war parties from Georgia continued their attacks on the few remaining tribes inhabiting the Paynes Prairie region until at last, by the 1730s, there was little remaining of the once powerful Timucua nation. It was at about this time that a young Creek warrior named Ahaya first rode with raiding parties into the La Chua region. The rich hardwood forests, fertile land, and abundant game, including herds of wild cattle descended from the La Chua stock, made quite an impression on the teenager.

Ahaya belonged to the Oconee tribe, named for the river in central Georgia on which they originally lived. While Ahaya was just an infant, the Oconees moved to the Chattahoochee River; it was there that the boy spent the remainder of his childhood. By his mid-twenties, Ahaya had been made chief of his village. Over the years, the young chief developed a passionate hatred for Spaniards, a fact noted with great appreciation by nearby English colonists. When James Oglethorpe launched an attack against St. Augustine in 1740, he didn't have any trouble recruiting Ahaya and thirty of his warriors. The invaders were unable to root out the Spanish from their fortress but did manage a little pillaging in the adjacent village.

Group outings such as this and increased contact with traders made the Creek lifestyle increasingly dependent on the white man. Instead of hunting only what was needed to keep their families fed, the Indians began taking large numbers of animals, mostly deer, whose hides were traded for guns, ammunition, ornaments, and other things that only the whites could provide. This new style of large-scale hunting required the men of the tribe to undertake lengthy trips to remote regions where game was plentiful. Paynes Prairie was an obvious choice and, with the added incentive of possibly capturing a stray Timucuan, it became the favorite destination for the Creek hunters.

The struggle between England and Spain for control of the Florida frontier was causing friction among the different Creek factions, who were often on opposing sides. Ahaya favored the English, who controlled Georgia, but didn't necessarily want to live near them. As the area became increasingly thick with colonists, the Oconee chief decided it was time to move. With rival Creek tribes to the west and English colonists to the north and east, Ahaya's choice for a new home was easy. He would move his people to the vacant La Chua region. Florida was still held by Ahaya's bitter enemies, the Spanish, but they had lost all interest in the interior.

Sometime around 1750, the Oconees moved. They set up a village on the south side of Paynes Prairie, possibly near the ruins of the Timucua village of Potano. In addition to the abundance of game and numerous lakes full of fish, there were the wild cows. The Indians built pens and then rounded up cattle from the surrounding countryside. His vast herds, compliments of his Spanish enemy, earned Ahaya the name "Cowkeeper."

It didn't take long for the newcomers to learn firsthand about Paynes Prairie's fickle nature. Shortly after their arrival, water filled the basin and remained long enough for fish to become well established. Then, about fifteen years after the Oconees' arrival, their new lake began to dry up. For a short while, the Indians enjoyed some easy fishing as the fish became crowded into shrinking water holes. But soon even the water holes began to dry and the fish died by the thou-

sands. Under the Florida sun, the ripening fish made the air around Paynes Prairie unbreathable.

The Oconees promptly moved their village to a new site, located several miles from the Prairie on the northwest shore of Lake Tuscawilla, where Micanopy now sits. They named the new village Cuscowilla. The Oconees' new home had all of the advantages of their former village on the Prairie and none of the smell.

For countless generations, the Oconees had been battling rival tribes and white settlers in Georgia, so now that they were neighbors with their hated enemies, the Spanish, it seemed only natural to undertake a campaign of raids. Choosing a target was easy. The majority of Spanish Floridians were all in St. Augustine, clinging desperately to their last stronghold on the mainland.

In 1757, Cowkeeper visited the governor of Georgia. He told the English governor that his occupation was making war on all Florida Indians who were allied with the Spanish. His obsessive hatred was reinforced by a vision he had in which he was told that to find peace in the great hereafter, he must kill one hundred Spaniards. By all accounts it would appear that he was anxious to meet his quota. The governor was grateful to have Cowkeeper's friendship. England at that time was at war with France for control of the North American frontier. During that struggle, known as the French and Indian War, Spain allied herself with France, which made Spanish Florida "enemy territory" to the English. For the Georgians, Cowkeeper's harassment of the enemy was welcome.

The French and Indian War ended in 1763 with Great Britain in control of most of North America east of the Mississippi River. Spain's prized possession, the island of Cuba, also fell to the English. To get it back, Spain was forced to turn over her claim to Florida. Cowkeeper could not have been happier and even traveled to St. Augustine to attend the inauguration of the new governor, Patrick Tonyn.

In the following months, other allied bands of Creeks came to meet with the new authorities in east Florida, but Cowkeeper, to demonstrate his independence, would not go at the same time. By 1771, the Oconees' desire to be dealt with as an independent tribe had earned them the name *semanolies,* which meant "wild people" or "runaways." In time the name evolved to Seminoles.

At about this same time, the name La Chua was also experiencing some evolution. When the British arrived, they changed it to "Alatchaway." In the following years, the name evolved through a series of variations such as "Elotchaway" and "Lotchoway" before the current name for the region, Alachua, finally emerged in the early 1800s.

Under British rule, the Seminoles enjoyed a period of relative calm. Traders began to make regular excursions into the interior, loaded down with guns, tools, and other products of European civilization for which the Indians would trade furs and pelts. In 1773, a company laid out an ambitious plan to establish trading posts at Paynes Prairie (known at that time as the Alachua Savanna), on the Suwannee River, and near Volusia, with a base on the St. Johns River near today's Palatka. But first, it had to get approval from the Seminoles. In 1774, two expeditions were sent inland, one to Cuscowilla and the other to Talahasochte on the Suwannee River, to meet with the local chiefs. In addition to a number of traders and representatives of the company, the expedition included a thirty-four-year-old naturalist named William Bartram, whose written account of the trip would make him and the Alachua Savanna famous.

William Bartram

William Bartram had no designs on being a great writer. He was a naturalist. At age fourteen, Billy, as he was known, joined his father on an exploration of the Catskill Mountains, where he first developed the love of nature that was to become his life-long passion. As a young man, he was encouraged by his father to be a businessman, but every enterprise he undertook failed, usually because he devoted too much time to exploring the local countryside.

In 1765, he again joined his father, John, a well-respected naturalist, on another exploration. In his newly acquired role of royal botanist to King George III, John Bartram was sent to explore England's newly acquired colony of East Florida. The expedition ended the following year, but William chose to remain in Florida and try his hand at running an indigo and cotton plantation. Again his business failed. He was forced to move back to his Pennsylvania homeland and for the next few years worked at several jobs. His break came in 1772, when a friend of his father, Dr. John Fothergill, offered William fifty pounds per year to gather plants, seeds, and other specimens of interest in Florida. He would receive extra pay for drawings of wildlife. Thus, the groundwork was laid for one of the most important explorations of the American Southeast. The resulting book, *Travels through North and South Carolina, Georgia, East and West Florida*, would become a cornerstone in the studies of the area's history, natural history, and literature.

Bartram set off from Pennsylvania in 1773, traveling southward through the Carolinas and Georgia. He eventually made his way to Spalding's Store, a trading post on the St. Johns River south of today's Palatka. In June 1774, he joined the traders heading for Cuscowilla.

When he first came within sight of the Alachua Savanna, Bartram was awestruck by what he called "the most sudden transition from darkness to light, that can possibly be exhibited in a natural landscape." He then gave a rich description, obviously enchanted at seeing the great savanna that, for so long, had taunted the imagination of the civilized world:

> The extensive Alachua Savanna is a level, green plain, above fifteen miles over, fifty miles in circumference, and scarcely a tree or bush of any kind to be seen upon it. It is encircled with high, sloping hills, covered with waving forests and fragrant Orange groves, rising from an exuberantly fertile soil. The towering *Magnolia grandiflora* and transcendent palm stand conspicuous amongst them. At the same time are seen innumerable droves of cattle; the lordly bull, the lowing cow and sleek capricious heifer. The hills and groves re-echo their cheerful, social voices. Herds of sprightly deer, squadrons of the beautiful, fleet Seminole horse, flocks of turkeys, civilized communities of the sonorous, watchful crane, mixed together, appearing happy and contented in their enjoyment of peace, 'til disturbed and affrighted by the warrior of man.

The party set up camp on the edge of Paynes Prairie. The next day, Bartram and the traders were honored with a great feast that featured a number of Cowkeeper's finest cattle, which had been rounded up and slaughtered that morning. It was a grand affair, but for Bartram it was an opportunity to study the Seminoles. Through his narrative, we get the only detailed description ever written of the first Seminole village.

> The town of Cuscowilla . . . contains about thirty habitations, each of which consists of two houses nearly the same size, about thirty feet in length, twelve feet wide, and about the same in height. The door is placed midway on one side or in the front. This house is divided equally across, into two apartments, one of which is the cook room and common

hall, and the other the lodging room. The other house is nearly of the same dimensions, standing about twenty yards from the dwelling house, its end fronting the door. The building is two stories high, and constructed in a different manner. It is divided traversely, as the other, but the end next the dwelling house is open on three sides, supported by posts or pillars. It has an open loft or platform, the ascent to which is by a portable stair or ladder: this is a pleasant, cool airy situation, and here the master or chief of the family retires to repose in the hot seasons, and receive his guests or visitors. The other half of this building is closed on all sides by notched logs; the lowest or ground part is a potatoe (sic) house, and the upper story over it a granary for corn and other provisions. Their houses are constructed of a kind of frame. In the first place, strong corner pillars are fixed in the ground, with others somewhat less, ranging on a line between; these are strengthened by cross pieces of timber, and the whole with the roof is covered close with the bark of the cypress tree. The dwelling stands near the middle of a square yard, encompassed by a low bank, formed with the earth taken out of the yard, which is always carefully swept. Their towns are clean, the inhabitants being particular in laying their filth at a proper distance from their dwellings, which undoubtedly contributes to the healthiness of their habitations.

The traders explained to Cowkeeper that William was interested in the local plants and animals. This amused the chief, who nicknamed Bartram *Puc Puggy*, "the Flower Hunter," and gave him permission to explore the area at will. Bartram wasted no time and for the next two days circumnavigated the Prairie and prowled the surrounding forest, collecting specimens and taking notes.

Of the many things he described, one of the most fascinat-

The Lost Village of Cuscowilla

O ne of the great unsolved mysteries of Florida archaeology is the location of Cuscowilla, the first Seminole
village. Although described in detail by William
Bartram and visited by many white traders and officials, the
town's exact location is unknown. What makes this especially
strange is that, while it was probably located within the present town limits of Micanopy, 175 years of determined archaeologists, farmers, gardeners, construction workers, and kids
with trowels have yet to uncover a single artifact that would
pinpoint Cuscowilla's exact location.

ing was the black wolf. Bartram's description of a wolf on
Paynes Prairie was the first on record of the animal, which
would later be known as the Florida red wolf. It became

Seminole chief Mico Chlucco, or the "Long Warrior,"
drawn by William Bartram. (Florida State Archives)

extinct in the early 1900s. But this was just one of many surprises Bartram gave the world in *Travels*. In all, he would describe nearly 125 new plant species and many animal varieties, including three snakes, six frogs, two lizards, six mammals, two or three fish, and over fifty birds. But for all of the questions he answered, he also created some mysteries. What, for instance, was the "painted vulture"? For many years, this question baffled ornithologists and in many cases fueled a mistrust of the accuracy of Bartram's accounts that prevailed in some circles for much of the nineteenth century. The current thinking is that the bird was a king vulture, which today is found only in the American Southwest. He also described what must have been an ocelot, but these small cats are not known to have been living any closer than Texas at the time.

When *Travels* was first published in 1791, its reception among scientific circles was cool. His descriptions seemed too fantastic to be true, and his colorful, enthusiastic style was quite different from the dry, matter-of-fact manner of presentation which, unfortunately, has always been expected of scientific writings. But the literary world loved it. Some of the more prominent writers of the budding Romantic period were completely enthralled by Bartram's book and tried to copy his

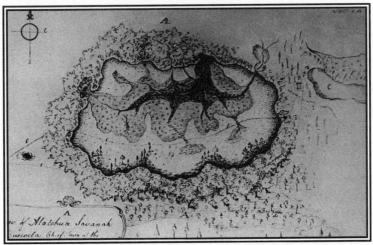

William Bartram's map of Paynes Prairie. (Florida State Archives)

style. In some of the works of Samuel T. Coleridge and William Wordsworth, Bartram's influence is unmistakable. François-René de Chateaubriand was so moved by Bartram's descriptions of the area that he used the Alachua Savanna and Cuscowilla as the setting for part of his famous story, *Atala,* published in 1801.

The Cuscowilla expedition was a complete success for everyone involved. By the time the trading party left Alachua for the store on the St. Johns, the traders had the Seminoles' permission to establish a post, the Indians had the promise of a steady supply of trade goods, and Bartram had a stack of detailed notes and drawings.

A Life-Saving Manuscript

Chateaubriand's accounts of his life were often as romanticized as his works of fiction. In 1792, while fighting in the siege of Thionville during the French Revolution, he was shot twice. He claimed his life was saved by his story of the great Alachua Savanna. Apparently, he was carrying the manuscript of *Atala* in his backpack during the battle and it stopped the two bullets.

Seminoles and the New Americans

Unfortunately for the Seminoles of Cuscowilla, the arrangements made with the traders would be short lived. Storm clouds were building to the north, where the wide-open expanses of North America had created an independent, strong-willed breed of people who were calling themselves, with increasing passion, "Americans." At the same time they were shaking off the grip of British rule, the American pioneers were relentlessly expanding their range. With the courage that comes from strength in numbers, the whites confidently built their homesteads wherever they found good land, even if it was already occupied by Indians.

American patriots on the Georgia frontier had heard about the legendary Alachua region. They were especially interested in Cowkeeper, not only because of the wealth of natural resources in his domain, but because of his staunch alliance with the English, who owned Florida. At the same time Bartram was visiting Cowkeeper's peaceful settlement, John Bryan, a patriot from Georgia, was busily scheming to gain control of it. Capitalizing on the friction between the Alachua Seminoles and their Creek relatives in Georgia, Bryan tricked some Creek chiefs into signing a land contract. The Indians were told that they were giving Bryan rights to set up a trading post. Instead, they signed over the title to several hundred thousand acres of their north Florida homeland.

Cowkeeper was stunned. Even though he was not on the best terms with his fellow Creeks in Georgia, he couldn't believe they had betrayed him. Soon, the colonial government became aware of Bryan's dealings and sought to rectify the problem. At a meeting with some of the Creek chiefs in 1774, Governor Wright of Georgia informed them that Bryan had tricked them. In anger, the chiefs tore their names from the treaty and stormed out of the talks. On their way back to their villages, the Indians ran into Bryan. Rather than shoot him on the spot, they calmly allowed the scoundrel to speak his peace. A short time later, after some fast talking and several bottles of whiskey, Bryan rode off with another treaty that said essentially the same thing as the first version.

When Governor Tonyn of Florida learned of the treachery, he ordered Chief Justice William Drayton to arrest Bryan. Drayton, however, had been involved in the scheme and helped Bryan to escape back to Georgia. In the end, the only thing Bryan could show for his efforts was a large red oak tree on the western edge of Paynes Prairie into which he had carved his name. Cowkeeper, on the other hand, had learned an important lesson about the new breed of Americans and the way they thought. William Bartram apparently was not an example of the way all Americans acted. Some were eager to explore the untamed wilderness while others wanted to own it.

Life on Paynes Prairie had been good to Chief Cowkeeper.

Healthy living and the occasional therapeutic raid had kept him in good shape, allowing him to reach almost seventy years of age. Still, there was one thing left unresolved. His quota of one hundred dead Spaniards, as required by his vision to attain everlasting peace in the great hereafter, had not yet been met. And with the severe shortage of Spaniards in the English-owned territory, the outlook was grim. But then, in 1783, the winds of change brought new hope for Cowkeeper.

As a result of Queen Anne's War, Britain turned control of Florida back to Spain. The news was a terrible blow for the Seminoles, but for the aged chief it was a chance for salvation. Cowkeeper mustered his strength and, with a band of his finest warriors, took the warpath. Unfortunately, the aged chief was more full of desire than strength. On the way to St. Augustine, Chief Cowkeeper fell ill. Tired and weak, he knew the end was near. As he lay dying, the chief called his two sons, Payne and Bowlegs, to his side. Recalling his vision of many years before, the chief informed them that he had succeeded in killing only eighty-six Spaniards. His fate was in their hands. It would be up to them to slay the remaining fourteen.

With Cowkeeper's death, the Seminole alliance with Britain weakened. The new leader, Payne, had come to realize that white allies were reliable only as long as it was in their best economic or political interest. He chose to adopt this same strategy. This became apparent in 1792 when William Augustus Bowles, a renegade British officer, attempted to carve an independent Seminole nation, called Muskogee, out of Spanish Florida. He hoped for Payne's support and on one occasion sought refuge for his small army at Paynestown. The chief refused. Later that year, Payne, along with his brother, Bowlegs, and White King of the Talahasochte Seminoles, led seven hundred warriors to the village of Miccosukee in an attempt to capture Bowles, but the would-be king of Muskogee had been warned and had escaped. The Seminoles were determined to guide their own destiny.

※

8. Newnan's Invasion

I n the years following Cowkeeper's immigration to Paynes
Prairie, many other bands moved into the state to escape
American persecution. Most were Creek Indians, but there
were other groups as well, including runaway black slaves. The
name Seminole, which had originally been given to Cowkeeper's
tribe at Paynes Prairie, was now used when referring to the
entire mix of Indians and blacks who now populated north
Florida. Cowkeeper's band was called the Alachua Seminoles.

Black refugees were nothing new in Florida. Since the late
1600s, slaves had been risking their lives to escape from their
English masters to the north and make their way to Florida, where
they could expect much kinder treatment from the Spanish. By
1739, there were so many black refugees in Florida, that a village
and fort, called Mose, were established for them a short distance
north of St. Augustine. The Spanish were grateful to have these
allies, who eagerly fought at their side when needed.

The Black and Indian Seminoles developed a relationship
that appeared to be slavery to white observers but was actually an alliance that benefited both groups. The Indians didn't
have anything against slavery; in fact, Cowkeeper himself was
served by captured Yamassee Indians when Bartram visited.

But the Indians realized that runaway blacks had more to offer as allies than as slaves. What developed was a relationship of mutual respect in which both sides had something to offer. For their part, the Indians had established a hold on the Florida interior and possessed a rich knowledge of the land. The blacks brought to the alliance an understanding of the white man's language and thinking processes. Together they formed a strong front against their mutual enemy, the Americans.

At Paynes Prairie, the blacks had their own villages near those of the Indians. They raised crops and had their own cattle, a portion of which was given as tribute to their Indian "masters." The arrangement was good for everyone except the white slave owners to the north, who were becoming increasingly outraged at the loss of their "property."

After Cowkeeper died, his son Payne became chief and, in hopes of gaining some badly needed respect from the Americans, took on the regal title of King Payne. King Payne moved his people to a site about two and a half miles northeast of Cuscowilla. The new settlement, called Paynestown, was located just west of today's Micanopy–Rochelle Road.

The morning of September 24, 1812, was typical for this time of year on Paynes Prairie. With the sun barely up over the horizon, the air was already warm and thick with humidity. At Paynestown, there was more activity than usual as nearly one hundred of King Payne's warriors prepared to leave with their chief on an expedition to St. Augustine. Shortly after sunrise, the band rode out of the village, heading north along the ancient Alachua Trail. By 8:30 A.M., the Indians passed the area of present-day Rochelle as they followed the path's northeast track. The easy pace allowed the eighty-year-old Payne to take in the quiet sounds of the forest. The magnificent groves of spreading oak trees, so easy to ride through, began giving way to stands of tall pines with a thick undergrowth of palmetto and wax myrtle. The old warrior and his great white stallion had traveled this ancient path countless times together over the years.

The Indians had just rounded a bend when the front of the

column erupted into a frenzy of horses dashing in all directions and warriors scrambling into the underbrush. As the path ahead of him cleared, King Payne could see, several hundred yards ahead, a large force of American soldiers. They too were frantically diving headlong into palmetto thickets and ducking behind pine trees. Of the few soldiers on horseback, one remained mounted, studying the Seminoles' movements and shouting commands. He was Col. Daniel Newnan, sent by the governor of Georgia to find the Alachua Seminoles and destroy them. Although he had been aware that he was in the Indians' territory, Newnan was caught off guard when he met them on the path.

The Americans had sent this army after the Alachua Seminoles to help eliminate the problem of runaway slaves and the occasional skirmishes that were erupting between Indians and settlers on the Georgia frontier. But their main goal was control of Florida. In an underhanded attempt to capture Florida, the American government unofficially supported a militia of Georgia and Florida citizens in an attack on Florida. The plan called for the militia to seize control of a section of Florida and then cede it to the United States government. The Patriot Rebellion, as this scheme was dubbed, began successfully with the easy capture of Fernandina. But at St. Augustine, all the patriotic fervor and expansionistic passion the militia could muster were no match for the stone walls of the Castillo de San Marcos. The invasion became a stalemate, with the American forces setting up a position outside the fort in a five-month siege. It was a miserable situation that was made worse by Bowlegs' leading his band of Alachua Seminoles on a series of raids against the Americans' rear flank. Annoying as this was, the Americans at last had an enemy they could engage in a battle. The task was assigned to Georgia militia Colonel Newnan.

On September 24, 1812, Colonel Newnan and an army of 117 soldiers, mostly volunteers from Georgia, left their camp on the St. Johns River and marched westward toward Alachua. Their orders were to burn the villages of the Alachua Seminoles, destroy or confiscate all of their possessions, and kill any Indian who could not be captured. The Americans were confident that they could easily defeat the Alachua Seminoles, but time was of the essence. As part of a militia, the soldiers were primarily volunteers, most of whom had only a few days left in their term of service. Newnan was forced to induce many of them to reenlist with the promise that they would be able to keep slaves and land captured during the invasion.

This was the type of offer that the Americans could appreciate. With renewed enthusiasm, 117 men were soon at Newnan's disposal, eager to rid the world of Seminoles. Some apparently had more ambition than good sense, marching into the Florida wilderness in bare feet. A few didn't even have guns. Newnan was so confident that the Indians could be quickly overrun and their supplies taken that he brought only four days' provisions and twelve horses. It was on their fourth day of travel through the Florida wilderness that Newnan's troops met their intended victims.

Payne's warriors wasted no time unslinging their packs from their shoulders and loading their weapons. Meanwhile, the Americans were advancing slowly and cautiously on foot. When the soldiers came to within two hundred yards, the Indians opened fire. Newnan ordered a charge. King Payne rode his horse back and forth through the ranks of his men, encouraging them and giving them inspiration as they bravely confronted the enemy. But even his bravery and experience weren't enough to keep the eighty-year-old warrior out of the way of flying bullets. Badly wounded, the chief was taken by some of his warriors back to the village.

On the battlefield, the Seminoles were slowly being forced back by the accurate shooting of the Georgian volunteers. After retreating about half a mile, the Indians reached a swamp where they were able to make a stand. Newnan realized that rushing the well-protected Indians would be suicidal, so he ordered his men to erect a log breastwork. As some of the soldiers cut logs, the rest kept the Indians back with a steady volley of bullets. A couple of the braver warriors ventured out from the swamp's protective cover, only to discover firsthand the deadly marksmanship for which the Georgia frontiersmen were famous. Some of the white soldiers made their way to the dead Seminoles and relieved them of their scalps, a final indignity that was standard procedure in frontier warfare for whites and Indians alike.

The standoff lasted the rest of the day. In the meantime, word of the fighting spread like wildfire to the villages of the Indians and the nearby black settlements around Paynes Prairie, and by late afternoon nearly one hundred warriors had arrived, doubling the Seminole force. Among them were Bowlegs and warriors from his village near Wacahoota, about ten miles southwest of Paynestown.

As they lay hidden in the swamp, the Indians painted their faces with war paint and made plans for an attack. About half an hour before sunset, they emerged, howling and screeching wildly like creatures of the forest. In the lead was Bowlegs, walking on his haunches and gyrating wildly as he approached the soldiers' breastwork. When the Indians got about two hundred yards away, they began shooting at the soldiers while continuing to advance. Not wanting to waste ammunition, Newnan's men restrained themselves until the Indians came within a comfortable range, and then they opened fire. By eight o'clock, the Indians were once again huddled in the swamp. So far, they had lost ten warriors but had been able to kill only three of their attackers.

With Indians scattered throughout the woods on all sides, the soldiers were unable to leave the protection of their breastwork. Throughout the night, they strengthened it and created portholes from which to fire their rifles. Their situation was desperate. That night a rider was sent back to St. Augustine for reinforcements. Six other soldiers decided to follow his example, jumped onto the six best horses, and rode away, leaving over a hundred of their comrades stranded in the wilderness with only five horses.

For the next couple of days, the soldiers remained trapped within the protection of their wooden breastwork with very little sign of the Seminoles. On the third day, the Indians returned and began taking random shots at the soldiers from a safe distance. This continued for another five or six days. The volunteers began talking openly of desertion as their hunger grew. In desperation, they shot one of the horses and quickly devoured it.

The Seminoles now realized that the soldiers had a fair supply of meat in the four remaining horses, so several warriors sneaked in and shot the animals. The soldiers would now have to eat their fill, for they had no way of preserving the horsemeat. This was the final blow. Colonel Newnan knew that he must escape or starve. Preparations were made, and at about nine o'clock that night the Georgians slipped out of "Fort Newnan." The Indians didn't fire a shot. Either they didn't see the soldiers or, more likely, they were just glad to see an end to the ordeal.

Weary from hunger, the tattered band groped their way through the woods. After only eight miles, the soldiers could go no further. The men used what little strength they had to build another breastwork alongside the path. Here they rested for a day before resuming their retreat to the St. Johns River. Other than one small skirmish with another small band of Seminoles, Newnan's troop managed to reach safety unharmed.

There is an ironic footnote to this story. About two hours

"Fort Newnan," where Daniel Newnan and his soldiers remained under siege by King Paynes' Seminoles for nearly a week, was nothing more than a breastwork of logs similar to the one shown in this drawing from John Frost's Life of Jackson *(1848). (Florida State Archives)*

after the Americans abandoned Fort Newnan, twenty-five mounted dragoons (cavalrymen) arrived to their rescue. Carrying fresh supplies and ammunition, the troop had come from the east along a path that closely parallels today's Hawthorne Road. Newnan, meanwhile, was heading northeast along the old Alachua Trail. Finding the structure empty, the horsemen, instead of following the path of their retreating fellow soldiers, turned around and headed back along the path on which they had come.

Back at Paynestown, the wounded King Payne held council with his brother, Bowlegs, and some of the other chiefs. Knowing that the humiliation they had just dealt the Americans would not go unanswered, they decided to abandon Paynestown and Bowlegs' village at Wacahoota. Bowlegs took his band west to the Suwannee River country, while Payne's band headed south. The bullet wound King Payne had received during the battle might have been little more than an inconvenience in his younger days, but he was now in his eighties and too weak to recover. Still hopeful for his people's future, he continued to hold councils to work out plans for peace as his condition worsened. Finally, two months after the battle at Newnans Lake, King Payne died.

After five months of preparation, the Americans launched another assault on Paynes Prairie. The Alachua Seminoles' decision to leave the area had proven to be a wise one. Unfortunately, some other bands of migrating Indians had settled in the abandoned Alachua villages, unaware of their mistake.

In February 1813, an army of 250 Tennessee volunteers rode down the Alachua Trail, headed for the Prairie. The fact that the immigrants encamped at Paynestown were mostly women, children, and older Indians didn't seem to bother the invaders, who killed several women and one old man. Some of the Indians managed to escape into the woods. From there they took potshots at the soldiers but were hardly more than a nuisance. For three weeks, the American soldiers looted and burned every village they could find between Paynestown and Wacahoota. Stolen horses were loaded down with stolen supplies. All crops were burned and cattle rounded up. Cattle that couldn't be taken were killed. In all, about sixty Indians lost their lives. One American was killed, and seven more were wounded. The Alachua Seminoles had been spared, but they would never again be able to have any significant settlements near Paynes Prairie, only scattered hamlets. This area was now the northern fringe of the Seminole domain but was still considered Seminole country and inaccessible to white settlers.

At St. Augustine, the Patriot Rebellion was collapsing. The American soldiers had pulled back to an encampment near the St. Johns River, and, in Washington, the U.S. government was finding it increasingly difficult to deny any responsibility for the invasion. In early May, the last of the patriots retreated to Georgia. The rebellion was over, but the spirit that had inspired it lived on in many of the Georgia frontiersmen.

On January 10, 1814, Buckner Harris led a small army of volunteers into Florida. Harris, a veteran of the failed Patriot Rebellion, was determined to seize Florida for the United States. He led his army southward, gathering volunteers along the way. When they reached Little Lake Bryant, east of today's Ocala in the Ocala National Forest, the patriots built Fort Mitchell. Their roster upon arrival numbered just over 100 but within a few months rose to nearly 160. Isolated in the remote outback of the Florida wilderness, they quietly proclaimed themselves rulers of the Independent Republic of East Florida. They then sent a dispatch to Washington, ceding their new republic to the United States. They were answered with a firm refusal by the U.S. government to aid their cause. The patriots were now truly isolated in a land belonging on paper to Spain and in reality to the Seminoles. With the murder of Buckner Harris by Indians on May 5, patriotic pride gave way to the more deeply rooted instinct to survive, and the fort was abandoned.

The patriots dispersed, but many of them either chose to stay in Florida or moved back within a few years. Some of their names—James Dell, Francis Sanchez, Joshua Stafford, and John Mizell—can be found in lists of the earliest settlers in the Paynes Prairie region.

Bowlegs was now hereditary chief of the Seminoles. Just as his brother had, Bowlegs favored the British. In 1814, Bowlegs and his warriors eagerly joined the British in their invasion

Mixed Loyalties at Fort Mitchell

The abandoned site of Fort Mitchell, where the patriots had struggled to gain Florida's admittance to the United States in 1814, was used fifty years later as a training ground for local Confederate soldiers intent on withdrawing Florida from that same Union.

against the American forces in the Battle of New Orleans. The attack failed, leaving Bowlegs with nothing to show for his efforts but the bitter hatred of Andrew Jackson. In 1818, Jackson led a campaign against the Seminole villages of north Florida in what we know today as the First Seminole War. His last stop was Bowlegs' village on the Suwannee River, which he reduced to ashes. Bowlegs escaped but died a short time later of unknown causes.

❧

9. Wantons
&

A ndrew Jackson's 1818 campaign against the Seminoles
had minimal effect on Florida. The territory still
belonged to Spain, and the Seminoles still controlled the
interior. The Indians had come through both the Patriot
Rebellion and Jackson's invasion as strong as ever, with waves of
immigrants swelling their numbers every year. Their main settlements were now primarily to the south, but Seminole
encampments and hunting parties were still common around
Paynes Prairie.

One result of the revolt was that Spain realized how weak her
hold on Florida was. With pressure coming from all along the
northern border, the interior was vulnerable as long as it remained
unsettled. The Seminoles had been enticed into an uneasy alliance
with the Spaniards but were still not necessarily good neighbors.
Only a few of the bravest Spaniards and those most wanted by the
law were willing to risk settling in the interior.

To remedy this situation, the king of Spain allowed grants
of land to anyone willing to homestead. One huge tract, which
included Paynes Prairie, was granted to Don Fernando de La
Maza Arredondo in appreciation for his successful raising and
arming of troops to defend St. Augustine during the patriot
uprising. The Arredondo Grant formed a square, with its center

at today's Micanopy, and covered much of present-day Alachua County. Terms of the grant, which was given on December 22, 1817, required that two hundred families had to be settled on the property within three years. Arredondo's representatives quickly set up a company and went to work, recruiting settlers and parceling out the land.

In 1819, Spain ceded Florida to the United States. The steady flow of immigrating Americans had become more than the Spaniards could handle. Besides, Andrew Jackson's raid had demonstrated that the Americans were capable of taking the region by force whenever they wanted. The Spanish wisely decided to leave without further conflict. Meanwhile, confident that the U.S. government would honor the Spanish grants, agents for Arredondo were building an outpost to serve the prospective colonists. Edward M. Wanton and Horatio Dexter were put in charge of the enterprise. Both had spent many years as traders among the Indians and had gained their respect. Before the first tree was felled, they met with the Seminoles to explain their plans and seek the approval of the Indians and their new chief, Micanopy.

Micanopy, a young nephew of the late King Payne, was an unimpressive leader. Often described as being overweight and rather dim-witted, Micanopy would probably not have been the Seminoles' first choice for a chief if it had been decided by vote. But it wasn't. The title was a matter of inheritance, passed along matrilineal lines from the chief to his sister's son. For better or worse, Micanopy was chief of the Seminoles and it was his approval that Wanton and Dexter needed. It was a relatively easy task because the Seminoles had developed an appreciation for guns, tools, and other trappings of the white man's culture. The benefits of having a trading post close at hand outweighed any misgivings the Seminoles may have had about allowing a white settlement in their own backyard. Besides, their main settlements were now well to the south. Pilaklikaha, Micanopy's town, was nearly seventy miles away, near present-day Dade City. As a show of gratitude for the chief's consent, Wanton proposed to name the new town Micanopy in his honor.

Chief Micanopy. (Florida State Archives)

Arredondo attained a year-and-a-half-long extension on the grant requirements, and, in the fall of 1820, settlement began. John Smith and Patrick Lannam arrived on November 7 and immediately began clearing land and building two cabins. One of the structures, measuring fifteen by twenty feet, was a dwelling for themselves and the other settlers who were expected shortly. The other, twenty feet by thirty feet, was to serve as both a home for Wanton and as a store. By the following March, the completed buildings sat on top of the rise overlooking Lake Tuscawilla from the northwest, and Alachua County's oldest settlement was born.

A traveler through the region in August reported that the community was growing. In addition to the original newcomers lodge and Edward Wanton's home, where he lived with his wife and children, there was also a trading store, a kitchen, a corn house, and two servants cabins. At the same time, work was under way to improve the ancient Alachua Trail so it could more easily accommodate wagon traffic. Another important supply route was the old trail heading southeastward toward Volusia along which William Bartram had traveled a half century before. At Volusia, Dexter had a post, which served to keep the enterprise outfitted.

Every load of supplies sent to Micanopy presented a tough challenge. Where the trail cut through dry areas, the ground was sandy and soft. In the wet areas it was even softer. These miserable conditions inspired Dexter to find a water route into Alachua. After a considerable effort, logs were cleared from Orange Creek and the way was open. A shallow draft boat could now travel from the St. Johns River to Orange Lake by way of the Oklawaha River and Orange Creek. From the northwest corner of the lake, Micanopy was an easy five miles over land. Dexter was so pleased with the water route that in 1825 he became first in a long line of Floridians to propose a cross-Florida barge canal.

The tiny community grew slowly. Settlers from the North were enticed to move to Micanopy and the Paynes Prairie region with promises of free land. The only stipulation was that for ninety days they would work for nothing more than room and board. Then, after residing in the area for a year, they would be given fifty acres. In the fall of 1822, time ran out for terms of the Arredondo Grant to be met. Rather than the two hundred families required by the grant, Micanopy had something more like twenty. Nonetheless, the government was impressed by the effort and allowed the grant to stand.

One large section of the Arredondo Grant, consisting of nearly twenty thousand acres, was traded to Moses Elias Levy in exchange for some property he had near the east coast. Lake Wauberg, Chacala Pond, and most of Paynes Prairie were part of his new holdings. On the southwest corner of his land, about two and a half miles west of Micanopy, Levy built Hogmasters Lakes Plantation, named for the lakes we now know as Levy and Ledwith. There he raised corn and other crops, but his main focus was on sugarcane, which was processed on the property in his own mill. He also tried some other crops with which he was familiar from his childhood in the Caribbean, but he had little success.

One of the plantation's most notable residents was Levy's son, David, who, using the family's original surname, Yulee, would later become a Florida Senator and an important figure in Florida's development. He was in school in Virginia, living with friends of his father, during the early years of his father's Paynes Prairie enterprise. In 1827, Moses Levy abruptly ended his financial support for David's education, leaving the boy, now seventeen, no choice but to move to his father's plantation. He spent the next four years helping run the operation. He then moved to St. Augustine in 1831, where he studied law and eventually began his political career.

Moses Levy's interest in developing his lands in the Alachua region was more than just economic. He was Jewish and for many years had dreamed of establishing a colony in Florida for his people. As soon as he acquired the land in Alachua, Levy embarked on a recruiting campaign, which took him to many cities in the Northeast and also to Europe. On an earlier trip to London in 1816, he had met a German Jew named Frederick Warburg, who was in England on behalf of several German families interested in settling in America. Their main interest was in trying to grow grapes for wine. The only problem, as far as Levy was concerned, was that the Germans were of a variety of races and religions. But in 1821, when the U.S. took control of the Florida territory, clearing the way for settlement, Levy's desire to develop his holdings overshadowed his religious ambitions. He sent a message to Warburg, inviting him to bring the Germans to Florida. They arrived in 1821.

The new village, called Pilgrimage, was situated near the southwest corner of Paynes Prairie. In addition to the German vintners, there were families from other parts of Europe and the northern U.S. By February 1822, this settlement was larger than Wanton's. An eyewitness account by Dr. William Simmons of St. Augustine reported about thirty people living in Pilgrimage in 1822, eight or nine of whom were white. There was also a third settlement headed by Colonel Haines, and two other settlements were under way. Many of the Europeans in Pilgrimage had definite ideas of what paradise should be. Most important, there had to be plenty of grapes with which to make wine. Vineyards were planted, but Florida's climate and soil proved to be unsuitable. Some of the newcomers were able to change their strategy and remain, while others headed for home.

By 1822, enough settlers had moved into Florida to gain it the status of a U.S. territory. Two years later, in 1824, Alachua County was created. It stretched from the Georgia border to near Tampa. Wanton's house in Micanopy had become the community center for all important meetings in the region. At one meeting, shortly after the county was created, local leaders decided that Newnansville would be made the county seat. Until preparations were made at Newnansville (today a ghost town near Alachua), all county business was conducted at Wantons.

A major factor in the decision to make Newnansville the county seat was that the newly built Bellamy Road passed through it. Completed in 1826, Bellamy Road connected St. Augustine to Pensacola and opened up much of northern Florida for overland travel and shipping. In the Alachua region, westbound travelers on the Bellamy Road went through the present-day locations of Melrose, Orange Heights, and Waldo before coming to Newnansville, just north of today's Alachua.

While Wanton continued to call his new hamlet Micanopy, the rest of the world was calling it Wantons, or "the intended settlement of Micanopy." Slowly and stubbornly, the consensus changed to suit Mr. Wanton. When the first post office was set up by the army on March 26, 1826, the matter was dealt with quite diplomatically. Isaac Clark, the new postmaster, listed the station as "Wantons—alias Micanopy."

As the sounds of chopping axes and grating saws echoed through the woods, heralding the arrival of civilization at Paynes Prairie, there were other efforts being made to tame the Florida wilderness. On September 18, 1823, a handful of American soldiers and Seminole chiefs met at a camp alongside Moultrie Creek near St. Augustine. There, a treaty was signed that set aside a huge portion of the peninsula for the Seminoles to call home.

*According to local legend, the old "Council Oak" in Micanopy
was the setting for many rendezvous between white
settlers and Indians in the early 1800s.*
(Florida State Archives)

The rest of the territory was open to white settlers. Unable to write, the Indians merely touched the pen to give their endorsement of the treaty. That touch of a pen, along with some modifications the following year, set the northern boundary of Seminole lands about twenty miles to the south of Micanopy.

In 1823, the Senate ratified the treaty, and by the end of the following year, a growing number of prospective colonists were inspecting and settling into the new, improved, Indian-free Alachua County. The transition was slow and there were still some small bands of Seminoles scattered around the countryside, but they tried to keep their distance except when trading. One small Seminole village, called Hogtown, sat alongside the creek that today bears its name (near present-day Westwood Middle School). It was a good location. Too good, in fact, because it wasn't long before a handful of settlers, looking for a spot to homestead, found the site, liked it, and began building several log cabins close to those of the Indians.

In 1824, as part of the Moultrie Creek agreement, north Florida's Seminoles and the other bands living in the region received payment of ten dollars for each Indian household for "improvements." And as far as the U.S. government was concerned, the only way an Indian could "improve" his household was to abandon it. At Hogtown, Chief John Mico, nicknamed the "Hogdriver," received twenty dollars on behalf of his village. Likewise, Chief Coosetimico received fifty dollars for his village at Orange Lake; for his village in San Felasco Hammock, Chief Chepano Hajo was given one hundred dollars. There is no further record of Chief John Mico or the Hogtown Seminoles, so we can assume that they abandoned their village and moved to the reservation.

With the Indians gone, Alachua's reputation as a natural paradise grew. For those adventurous souls who decided to start a new life here, however, it soon became apparent that living in paradise had its price.

❧

10. *The Second Seminole War*

In September 1823, Governor Duval met with about seventy of the Seminole leaders to work out an agreement that would prevent hostilities between the white immigrants and the Indians. Both populations were growing and finding it hard to avoid each other. In the past, such treaties had been little more than a theatrical way of presenting the Indians with an ultimatum. But at the seventeen-day meeting held along the banks of Moultrie Creek near St. Augustine, there appeared to be a genuine willingness to negotiate. In fact, some of the whites present might actually have believed that any agreements made would be honored by the U.S. government. Others knew full well that they would not be.

Not all the Seminoles were taken in by the proceedings. Only thirty-two of the Indians present on this occasion—less than half—were willing to put their mark on the document, but that was more than enough as far as the Americans were concerned. The agreement, known as the Treaty of Moultrie Creek, required the Indians to stay within a four-million-acre reservation in the peninsula's interior. The Indians also agreed to turn over any runaway slaves living among them. This stipulation turned out to be as open to creative interpretation as the reservation boundaries themselves. In return, the whites were to stay off the reservation except for legitimate reasons. Upon moving, the Indians were paid a total of $4,500 for the abandoned lands. At the reservation, they were given $6,000 worth of tools and livestock, $2,000 for transportation, $1,000 per year for a school, and $1,000 per year for a blacksmith and gunsmith. In addition, for each of the twenty years that the treaty was to be in effect, the tribe was to receive $5,000.

The Indians turned over all runaway slaves, but there were still many blacks among the Seminoles whose families had been living with the Indians for nearly half a century. They were as much a part of the Seminole mix as the Indians themselves. As of 1808, no more blacks could be shipped to the U.S. from Africa as slaves. To an economy that relied heavily on slave labor, this gave new importance to the slaves already here, for they would now have to be the "breeding stock" of all future generations of slaves. Slave raiders made illegal forays into Seminole country, capturing every dark-skinned person they could find. If the captive hadn't been a slave before, he was now. In general, the settlers approved of the slave raiders and anyone else who could diminish the native population.

The Seminoles weren't too concerned with the reservation boundaries either, but their motivation was more basic—they were starving. What little food they managed to grow on the poor soil was destroyed by a severe drought in 1826. Governor Duval, realizing that the frontier was teetering on the edge of disaster, ordered the establishment of a military post near the northern extreme of the reservation. Fort King was built in 1827 near the present town of Ocala. Soon afterwards, Duval made an inspection of the reservation. He wrote, "The best of the Indian lands are worth but little; nineteen twentieths of their whole country within the present boundary is by far the poorest and most miserable region I ever beheld." The Seminoles tried hard to keep within the bounds, but it proved impossible.

For several years the tension built. Councils were held and threats made. But there was no getting around the fact that both the Seminoles and Americans were equally determined to live in central Florida. In 1829, Andrew Jackson became president. Like a bad dream, the Seminoles' most determined adversary was back, and once again he was in a position to act on his passionate hatred of them. One of his first presidential acts was to push for legislation requiring the Indians to move to lands set aside for them west of the Mississippi. Otherwise, they would come under the jurisdiction of the Florida Territorial Government and be subject to all of its laws. On May 28, 1830, that legislation was passed.

It wasn't until 1832 that Col. James Gadsden arranged a council with the Seminoles, during which the ultimatum was presented. This agreement, known as the Treaty of Paynes Landing, said that in addition to remaining a self-governing tribe, the Seminoles would receive $80,000 in cash and grants if they would make the move. If they stayed, supplies might be cut off and they would be subject to Florida territorial law. Seven of the chiefs' signatures wound up on the treaty but it is not clear how. Soon after the meeting adjourned, charges of coercion and forgery were leveled by some of the chiefs. Forgery was particularly easy with the Indians since they were unable to write and never actually signed their names. A chief's name would be written on the document by one of the Americans, and then the chief in question touched the pen to signify his consent. Micanopy was one of the chiefs whose name mysteriously appeared on the parchment.

The treaty also stipulated that a delegation of chiefs had to inspect and approve the new lands set aside for them. The Indians went and were not impressed. Nevertheless, their signatures again found their way onto the document, and a deadline for removal was set. Conferences continued to be held, but they were becoming little more than formal gripe sessions punctuated by American demands that the Indians move west.

The whites were determined to rid Florida of the Seminoles, and most of the Seminoles were equally determined to stay. Runaway blacks who made their way to the Seminole villages were given sanctuary, contrary to the rules established at Moultrie Creek. The settlers in Alachua County became impatient, and in 1833, ninety of the county's most prominent citizens signed a petition expressing their anger over the Indians' reluctance to turn over runaway slaves.

At one of the council meetings in 1834, a new face appeared. He was a handsome young warrior who was only a minor chieftain, yet his sway over the other leaders and his passionate objection to moving west got the attention of everyone present. His name, Osceola, was one they would come to know well. In May 1835, Osceola and the Indian agent at Fort King, Wiley Thompson, got into a heated argument. Thompson had the furious warrior dragged to the stockade and put in irons. When he cooled off, Osceola humbled himself to Thompson and was released. As a show of good will, or perhaps because he realized he had just made a huge mistake, Agent Thompson gave Osceola a rifle. The warrior accepted the gift, probably knowing in his heart that one day he would use it on Thompson.

Hostilities Begin

Confrontations along the frontier were becoming increasingly violent. Then, in June 1835, the first blood was shed. A party of eight Seminoles left the reservation to hunt near Paynes Prairie. Word of the Indians' presence reached Spring Grove, a small settlement near the present-day intersection of I-75 and Newberry Road. A mounted posse of local farmers called the Spring Grove Guard had recently been organized for just such an occasion. Now their moment had come.

Under militia Maj. Llewellyn Williams, seven members of the Guard rode south toward the Prairie, where they soon picked up the Indians' trail. On June 19, six of the Seminole hunters were found at Hickory Sink, just west of Lake Kanapaha. In keeping with age-old standards of frontier justice, the militiamen began doling out punishment with their cattle whips. At about that time, the two other Indians showed up and promptly opened fire on the whites. In the commotion, the six captives managed to escape into the woods. Two of them were shot during the skirmish, one fatally. Three of the

Osceola. (Florida State Archives)

Guards were wounded, but none died.

The Seminoles were outraged by the incident. Two months later, in what Gen. Duncan Clinch felt was an act of revenge, six Seminoles ambushed and killed a mail carrier near Tampa Bay. Realizing that they would have to make a stand, the Seminole leaders gathered in the safety of the watery region they called Tsala Apopka. The whites called it the Big Swamp, but it is the Indian name for the area that is used today. At Tsala Apopka, it was decided that any Seminole who made preparations to move west would be killed.

On November 30, 1835, Seminole leader Charley Emathla went to Fort King to sell his cattle in preparation to emigrate. He had always spoken in favor of relocation and was aware that his position would no longer be tolerated by his fellow Seminoles. At Fort King, he mentioned to the Americans that he felt his life was in danger. He was right. As he made his way home, twelve warriors led by Osceola ambushed Emathla and killed him. To show their disdain for everything American, the Indians took the money Emathla had been carrying and threw it into the air, allowing it to fall around his corpse. For weeks, passing Indians would not go near the dead man for fear of appearing sympathetic and therefore suffering the same fate. Eventually, a passing troop of soldiers buried Emathla's corpse.

In mid-November, sensing that war was inevitable, General Clinch became concerned for his plantation, which lay about ten miles south of Micanopy. He ordered half the garrison from nearby Fort King to move to his property. The Auld Lang Syne Plantation would now be secure. In the months that followed, the new stronghold, named Fort Drane, would become the closest thing possible to hell on earth. Clinch's concern was not entirely unfounded. He had created many enemies among the Seminoles when, in 1814, he blew up Negro Fort, a stronghold of free blacks and Indians on the Apalachicola River. Only about sixty of over three hundred occupants survived the explosion, and many of those were now in the ranks of the hostile Seminoles. One, a black named Abraham, was advisor to Micanopy and was considered the driving force behind many of the dull-minded chief's actions.

Clinch wasn't the only one who felt the need to fortify. Colonel McIntosh directed the construction of a fort on his nearby Oakland Plantation near Orange Lake. Throughout the Alachua region, homesteaders were strengthening their homes and erecting stockaded fences around them to provide safety for their families and neighbors. Wanton's post at Micanopy was stockaded and made a primary base from which the army could deal with the Indians. The stronghold was named Fort Defiance.

Another stockade was built on the property of Mr. Tarver, just east of Alachua Sink. Perched on Skeleton Hill, the finest overlook on Paynes Prairie, Fort Tarver became a favorite gathering place for American troops as well as local residents during Indian scares. From this vantage point a few months later, the residents of Fort Tarver would witness the Battle of Black Point, marking the beginning of the Second Seminole War.

The stage was set on December 17, with a couple of raids

Micanopy's advisor, Abraham. (Florida State Archives)

on the plantations of Colonel Simmons of Micanopy and Captain Priest near Wacahoota. No one was hurt, but some damage was done and the Seminoles made off with a number of cows. The next day, militia Colonel Warren, who had about 150 militiamen at Fort Crum on the western margin of Paynes Prairie, was instructed by General Clinch to scout the area. In the woods just west of the Prairie, he split his force. Captains McLemore and Lancaster were sent ahead toward Wacahoota, while Warren took a detachment of men and three supply wagons along the southern edge of Paynes Prairie, headed for Micanopy. As they passed below Bolen Bluff, where U.S. Highway 441 now leaves the Prairie, they were attacked by eighty Seminoles led by Osceola.

Having received word of the fight, Captain McLemore charged onto the scene with thirty militiamen. When they saw the number of Indians they were up against, most of the settlers turned their horses and rode away. It was a wise move but one that was not much appreciated by the twelve brave souls who chose to stay and fight.

After a brief battle, Osceola's band rode away with all of the soldiers' supplies and ammunition. The ravaged band of militia gathered up their dead and wounded and made their way back to Fort Crum. There, the dead were buried and the wounded soldiers treated. Two of the more seriously injured died a short time later, bringing to eight the final death count of the Battle of Black Point.

A few days later, militia Brig. Gen. Richard Keith Call led an army of soldiers toward Micanopy in search of the renegades. When they reached Malachai Hogan's property, near the old site of Paynestown, they found the settler's house in flames. The soldiers spotted several Seminoles dashing into the nearby underbrush and rode hard after them. They finally caught up at a small pond called Black Pool. Five of the Indians were killed while the rest managed to escape. Of the loot that the Indians had captured at Black Point, only a few papers were recovered.

War had begun and Osceola was not going to wait for the Americans to strike. The supplies captured from Warren's convoy at Black Point were just what Osceola needed to turn the talk of war into action. On December 28, 1835, Osceola and a handful of warriors crept up behind some trees outside of the Indian agency at Fort King. Osceola knelt in the scrub, clutching the rifle that Agent Thompson had given him some months before. The rifle had served as a constant reminder of the humiliation he had suffered at Thompson's hands, and with it he was now prepared to get his revenge. After dinner, Thompson decided to take a stroll outside of the pickets. This would be his last bad decision. A sudden volley of gunfire from the Seminoles left Thompson and his aide dead where they fell. The Indians then promptly removed Thompson's scalp and divided it among themselves.

On the same day, Chief Micanopy, leading 180 warriors, ambushed a column of soldiers sent from Fort Brooke near present-day Tampa to reinforce Fort King. In a stand of pines near present-day Bushnell, the Indians opened fire from palmetto thickets adjacent to the path. Nearly half of the soldiers fell in the first round of gunshots. Popular accounts of the battle credit Micanopy with the shot that killed the troop's leader, Maj. Francis Dade. Only three soldiers managed to escape the slaughter, which history has labeled the Dade Massacre. Of those, only Ransome Clarke survived to tell the story of the ambush.

In answer to a call for volunteers, many young men from the Alachua region joined the militia under the leadership of Governor Richard Keith Call. Most joined in August for a four-month tour of duty, meaning their term would expire on New Year's Eve. Call knew that if he was going to launch a strike, it would have to be soon. On Christmas Eve 1835, Call and 560 Florida frontiersmen arrived at Fort Drane on General Clinch's plantation. On December 29, they joined a force of 250 regulars under Clinch and marched toward a Seminole stronghold near the Withlacoochee River.

Upon reaching the river's north bank, they found the water too deep to ford, so they were forced to use an old, leaky Indian canoe lying nearby. Clinch had just crossed with all of his regulars when the woods erupted in Seminole gunfire. For over an hour, the soldiers remained pinned down by the hail of Indian bullets, aided by only sixty volunteers, who were able to cross the stream to join in. Finally a log bridge was built, allowing a retreat to the river's north bank. Three Indians and four whites lost their lives in the skirmish. Battered and out of supplies, the soldiers made their way back to Fort Drane.

At Fort Drane, another kind of battle was begun, a battle of words and accusations between the regular soldiers and Florida's volunteer militia. The fact that most of the volunteer force had remained on the north bank during the fight brought a flood of accusations, primarily that the Floridians had not joined the fray because their tour of duty was to end the following day. Governor Call defended his men, saying that they had stayed put on his orders, which were given in an attempt to cover the army's flank. The Floridians also had complaints. They accused the army of

Duncan Clinch. (Matheson Historical Center)

being ill prepared and of supplying only enough rations to last until the volunteers' service ended on New Year's Day. This bickering between regulars and militia was not entirely new and would continue through the course of the war, each faction feeling the other was inferior in battle.

In Washington, news of the fighting in Florida fueled the government's determination to eliminate the Seminole problem, by force if necessary. Gen. Winfield Scott was sent to take charge of the Florida campaign. He planned a three-pronged attack on the Cove of the Withlacoochee (known today as Lake Tsala Apopka), where the Indians were thought to be gathered. At the same time, Gen. Edmund Pendleton Gaines, commander of the Western Department, which included part of the Seminole domain, decided to lead his own attack on the Indians. He brought his force northward from Tampa Bay toward Fort King, where he hoped to find supplies. Along the way, they passed the scene of the Dade Massacre, pausing long enough to bury the dead soldiers, whose bodies had been left untouched for nearly two months.

At Fort King, Gaines was disappointed to find none of the rations he had expected. He had no choice but to return to Fort Brooke at Tampa Bay. But rather than return by the same road, he chose a route that would pass the scene of Clinch's battle on the Withlacoochee and perhaps give him a chance to find the Seminoles.

On February 27, 1836, one day after leaving Fort King, Gaines' force reached the Withlacoochee near Clinch's battlefield. It wasn't long before Gaines' wish to encounter the Seminoles was realized. It was late in the day so Gaines ordered his men to make camp. The next morning, he moved his force cautiously downstream until they came to a good crossing. An advance party was ordered to cross the river; upon entering the water, their leader, Lt. James Izard, was fatally shot in the head. With this, the Seminoles attacked in earnest, and by day's end, under heavy gunfire, Gaines had to order the construction of a log breastwork. This structure would be home to Gaines' men for the next eight days as they remained besieged by the Indians.

On March 6, with both sides growing tired of the siege, a meeting was arranged. Chiefs Jumper, Alligator, and Osceola met with emissaries from Gaines' camp and tried to negotiate an end to the hostilities. As the meeting was under way, General Clinch arrived with reinforcements and, unaware of the negotiations, attacked the Indians. The Indians dispersed, and General Gaines' beleaguered troops accompanied Clinch's soldiers to the relative safety of Fort Drane.

A Tale of Two Sieges

When General Gaines decided to lead his campaign against the Seminoles, he did so in defiance of an order from Washington instructing him to go to Texas, where trouble was brewing with the Mexicans. During the same eight days that Gaines' men were kept under siege, the Texans they were supposed to be helping also were besieged in a small church called the Alamo in San Antonio. On March 6, 1836, the same day that Gaines' siege ended, the thirteen-day siege of the Alamo also ended, with a massacre in which only 4 of 167 occupants survived.

The Paynes Prairie region was now totally void of all but the most stubborn settlers, the majority of whom were crowded into the larger towns, such as Jacksonville, St. Augustine, and Newnansville. Newnansville, today a ghost town near the town of Alachua, was a fair-sized frontier community and the Alachua County seat when the war started. With its population swollen by refugees, Newnansville's economy boomed.

An army doctor named Jacob Motte wrote an interesting account of the region when he came through in 1837. In his book, *Journey into Wilderness*, he described Newnansville as a community with a mix of mansions and shanties constructed along a "labyrinth of streets and lanes, laid out with a pleasing disregard to all rules of uniformity." His enjoyment of the city was tempered by a mild contempt for the uncivilized woods folk who now crowded the streets. He wrote, "The sudden increase of population and consequent prosperity to the incipient city was caused entirely by the innate dread and very natural dislike of its inhabitants to being scalped. They were mostly small farmers who had emigrated from different states and settled in Alachua county to plant corn, hoe potatoes, and beget ugly little white-headed responsibilities."

Motte went on to say that it was the general opinion that the settlers intentionally instigated hostilities and then "built pickets or stockades which they called forts, drew rations as they designated themselves 'suffering inhabitants' and devoted their attention entirely to the last of their former occupations. Finding this a very agreeable way of living, they occasionally united together, and riding through the country in strong parties, managed to kill a stray Indian or two." This, he wrote, was suspected of being an intentional effort to keep the war going. Other documents of the time confirm that this was a widely held opinion.

The old town of St. Augustine was caught off guard by the outbreak of hostilities. People from across the region flocked to the shelter of the massive Castillo San Marcos. But they weren't as safe as they thought. Almost all of the gunpowder in town had recently been sold to the Seminoles.

After the two battles along the Withlacoochee, the war settled into a pattern of random Seminole attacks on homesteads and small army patrols. The soldiers at Fort Drane were getting a full dose of Florida's summer weather. The sun bore down on them while sniping Indians, ravenous insects, and diseases such as yellow fever and malaria made the fort a truly miserable place. Even the seasoned chief surgeon of the fort found the deluge of sick soldiers unbearable. His assistant, John Bemrose, related that the doctor "had a great liking for the lancet [a small surgical knife]: he seemed to feel he got rid of the patients the more readily." But despite the doctor's efforts, the sick list grew. Available space was used up, and it became necessary to build a long lean-to type of shelter along the outside of the fort's north wall. Bemrose described it as "150 yards in length, a mere temporary affair covered only with bark, and letting in at the many cracks both sun and rain." Those men who managed to avoid infection were forced to entertain themselves within the fort's walls. The alternative was a foray into the surrounding woods to hunt or to pick some of the melons that Clinch had planted earlier in the year. But the risks were high. Seminoles kept an almost constant vigil from the surrounding woods.

At Micanopy, things were not much better. Both the Indians and the elements had been as brutal to the Paynes Prairie stronghold as they had to Fort Drane and the other posts during the summer of 1836. On June 9, Maj. Julius Heilman had to take action against about 250 Seminoles, supposedly led by Osceola, who had been harassing Fort Defiance from the nearby Tuscawilla Hammock. Heilman sent his men out in a three-pronged pincer movement, which effectively contained the Indians. From the fort, Heilman could see the action was going well. Caught up in the excitement, he charged out of the fort, accompanied only by a small cannon and its devoted crew. With their six-pounder blazing away, the little Heilman squad scattered the astonished Indians. Their assault lasted until they learned that the fort was being threatened and needed its cannon back. The major returned with his squad to the fort, leaving the infantry and mounted dragoons to finish driving off the Indians.

Major Heilman survived the skirmish at Tuscawilla Hammock intact, but he had apparently used up his quota of good luck. Two days later, he moved his headquarters to the disease-infested Fort Drane, and by the end of the month he was dead of malaria.

On June 19, 1836, with over a third of its inhabitants sick with malaria, Fort Drane was evacuated to Micanopy. The first phase of the move consisted of sixty men and a train of twenty-two wagons carrying ammunition and supplies. The column stretched for about five hundred yards as it approached Micanopy's Fort Defiance. When they were within a quarter mile of the fort, the soldiers came under fire from Osceola and two hundred warriors. The whites were badly outnumbered but managed to hold their own until a band of thirty soldiers arrived from Fort Defiance and helped drive the attackers back into the woods. This fight, called the Battle of Welika Pond, cost five soldiers their lives and wounded six more.

The remainder of the garrison at Fort Drane was too weak to move without reinforcements. These finally arrived, 250 strong, and on August 7, 1836, the fort was abandoned along with the rest of Colonel Clinch's plantation, including twelve thousand bushels of corn, ripe in the field. Osceola and his warriors wasted little time moving in and setting up house at the deserted fort. The white soldiers had been thorough in their packing. The only thing they had left behind was disease. It was here that Osceola is thought to have contracted the malaria that eventually led to his death a year and a half later.

The soldiers who had evacuated Fort Drane didn't find conditions any better at Micanopy. Soon the futility of this situation became apparent, and orders were issued to evacuate Fort Defiance. The garrison at Fort King, near present-day Ocala, had been vacant since June 9, so, with Micanopy abandoned, the entire Florida peninsula would again be in Seminole control except for a few coastal outposts. The evacuation of Micanopy was to be carried out by Maj. B. K. Pierce.

When he reached Micanopy on August 20, 1836, Pierce learned about Osceola's band living in Fort Drane. The temptation was more than he could resist. He had not come prepared for battle, and his soldiers were infantry, with none of the horses necessary to launch a raid. He remedied this problem by unharnessing about fifty of the work horses used to pull wagons and mounting some of his inexperienced soldiers on them. Along with his draft-horse cavalry, Pierce brought fifty more of his soldiers on foot. The Seminoles were found and attacked at the cost of one white soldier's life and an undetermined number of Seminoles.

Pierce began evacuating Fort Defiance on August 24, 1836. Central Florida was now void of whites, and for the first time in over ten years, the Seminoles were able to hunt the woods around Paynes Prairie with very little concern for their safety. This lull in the hostilities proved to be little more than the eye of the storm. In a very short time, war would again batter the Florida frontier.

The War Resumes

Governor Richard Keith Call was given command of the forces in Florida on June 21, 1836. His strategy was to contain the Indians in the Withlacoochee wilderness by means of a four-pronged pincer movement. The idea won the favor of President Jackson, who, at this point, was willing to try anything. It was early September before Call could finally launch his campaign. He first sent an advance party of one hundred men under militia Col. John Warren to begin preparations. On September 18, as they traveled through the San Felasco Hammock, just to the northwest of present-day Gainesville, Warren's troops were attacked. The large band of Seminoles was able to make a good stand until some effective cannon fire sent them scrambling into the underbrush.

The vanguard of General Call's invasion also engaged in several small skirmishes. Then, on October 1, the general's main force moved quickly southward in an attempted surprise attack on Fort Drane. It was believed that the main body of hostile Indians was still enjoying the accommodations there, and Call hoped to catch them off guard. When the army arrived, they found the structure in ruins. The Seminoles may have learned of the impending attack, but it's more likely that when the Seminoles realized that the fort was infested with white men's diseases, they torched it.

Call's long-awaited chance to prove himself became a miserable failure. For a month, he tried to meet the Indians head on but was frustrated in all attempts. At last, from November 18–21, he finally got his fight at the Battle of Wahoo Swamp. It was an unimpressive effort, and Call's army was essentially defeated. President Jackson stripped him of his command.

The next commander to try his hand with the Seminoles was Gen. Thomas S. Jesup. On December 8, 1836, he took charge of the nearly two thousand soldiers then based in Florida. Col. Zachary Taylor, known for his creative tactics, proposed to Jesup that the state be divided into square districts of twenty square miles each. At the center of each section, a fort would be established to serve the residents. This would make the countryside safer and help troops in the field. Residents in the Paynes Prairie region, designated as District 7, would be served by a fort at Micanopy.

In the early spring of 1837, work began amidst the charred ruins of Fort Defiance to build the new fortress. This one was to be stronger and larger then its predecessor. It was dubbed Fort Micanopy and was formally established on April 30, 1837. One hundred forty-one men made up the fort's roster when it opened. From here the military could provide aid to the local population. Other smaller settlers' forts that had existed since hostilities first erupted, such as Fort Crum, remained to provide sanctuary for families in the immediate area. In addition, several new forts were erected in the Paynes Prairie region. Fort Walker was set up on Kanapaha Prairie, close to the site of the skirmish of 1835. On the other side of the Prairie, Fort Crane was built alongside the ancient Alachua Trail. Today, the hamlet of Rochelle lies just north of the site.

Near the Spring Grove settlement, a stronghold was built, which the residents called Fort Clark. Today, there is a small, roughly defined area, just west of I-75 on Newberry Road, that is called Fort Clark. Nothing remains of the wooden blockhouse that stood on or near the site now occupied by the Fort Clark Church on the south side of Newberry Road. A historical marker in the church's front yard explains the area's history and tells about the old fort.

During the summer of 1837, an end to the war seemed near. The Indians agreed to relocate to Oklahoma and were gathering in large numbers at Tampa Bay to await transportation. Micanopy, Jumper, Alligator, Coacoochee, and Abraham were among the chiefs who had camps set up near Fort Brooke. Osceola was predictably absent. General Jesup was so confident that the hostilities were nearly over that he sent most of the militia and volunteers home and shipped the marines north. Settlers were advised that all was safe and, since it was getting expensive to feed and shelter them, were encouraged to leave the forts.

All was going well until the slavers showed up at Fort Brooke. Contrary to the agreement that the Indians would be allowed to leave with their black brethren, white slavers began to visit the Seminole encampments looking for runaways. When Osceola learned of this, he wasted no time in coming to Fort Brooke. There, under cover of darkness, he smuggled all seven hundred Indians out of the encampment. The war was in full swing again, and the Alachua frontier folk were easy prey. They were forced to retreat, once again, to the forts. By the fall of 1837, Jesup had little to show for his efforts except a lot of burned villages and crops, dead livestock, and a number of hostages, mostly women, children, and cows. In desperation, he laid aside his honor and undertook a policy of shameless treachery that shocked and disgusted much of the nation.

On October 23, 1837, Osceola and Alligator arrived at Fort Peyton, near Moultrie Creek, with a number of warriors, hoping to negotiate the release of the recently captured subchief, King Philip. They set up camp near the fort and hoisted a white flag. Not long before, Jesup had supplied the Indians with many yards of white cloth to make such flags, which he had told them would indicate peaceful intentions and guarantee safe passage. General Jesup was reluctant to meet with the Indians, so he sent General Hernandez to do his dirty work. Jesup watched from the safety of Fort Peyton as Hernandez rode to the Indian camp. Instead of honoring the flag of truce, the soldiers seized Osceola and his band and marched them off to St. Augustine. Micanopy, Cloud, and eleven other chiefs went to meet with Jesup one month later, on December 3. They too were proudly displaying the white flag, as Jesup had instructed. They too were captured. Slowly but surely, the general was imprisoning all of the most powerful Seminole leaders.

The captive Indians were all taken to St. Augustine and held in the Castillo, which had been renamed Fort Marion shortly before the war. From there, destiny carried each of the Indians in a different direction. Some, including Coacoochee, managed to escape. Having persuaded their keepers to let them gather herbs in the nearby woods, some of the captive women were able to gather yaupon leaves with which they were able to make a batch of black drink. For many days the warriors fasted, consuming only the black drink, which among other things is a powerful diuretic, causing considerable weight loss. At last Coacoochee and seventeen other warriors had grown thin enough to squeeze through the narrow bars lodged in the one small window in their cell.

Most of the remaining captives wound up on a reservation in Oklahoma. Micanopy reached the Indian Territories, as the region was generally known, on June 12, 1838. There, he continued as nominal chief of the Seminoles until his death in January 1849. Osceola's fate was even worse. After Coacoochee's escape, Osceola was sent to Fort Moultrie at Charleston, South Carolina. He was still sick with the malaria he had contracted at Fort Drane a year and a half earlier. In his weakened state, other complications set in, and on January 31, 1838, he died at the age of thirty-five.

After Osceola's death, his head and body were separated and sent in different directions, beginning a tale too strange for fiction. Dr. Weedon, whom Osceola had considered a good friend, severed the young warrior's head and placed it in the coffin with his body. To conceal the wound, Dr. Weedon tied a scarf around the corpse's neck. Then, shortly before the coffin was to be unceremoniously buried outside the walls of Fort Moultrie, Dr. Weedon removed his trophy.

Studying the heads of different people was an accepted science in those days, based on the notion that certain characteristics of a person's skull were related to traits such as intelligence and aptitude. In Dr. Weedon's case, his methods of research seem almost tame in comparison to his methods of child rearing: when any of his three sons misbehaved, the good doctor would hang Osceola's head on the child's bedpost for the night. After the Weedon nursery, Osceola's head did a short stint as a novelty in the home of Dr. Weedon's son-in-law, Dr. Daniel Whitehurst. He, in turn, presented the gruesome trophy to Dr. Mott, who displayed it proudly in his Surgical and Pathological Museum in New York City. There it remained until 1866, when fire ravaged the collection, mercifully cremating Osceola's skull.

Coacoochee was now looked to for leadership by all of the Seminoles who were still determined to stay and fight. Steady pressure was forcing the Seminoles—and the war—continually southward. The last big battle of the war was fought on Christmas Day, 1837. Near the northeast edge of Lake Okeechobee, Coacoochee's warriors met a force of nearly eleven hundred soldiers under Col. Zachary Taylor in one of the bloodiest battles of the war. Almost everyone who emerged from the battle was wounded. Twenty-eight whites and ten Seminoles were killed.

The remainder of the Second Seminole War was characterized by small, random skirmishes. But even with the main body of Seminoles moving southward, the Alachua region was far from safe. There were still plenty of hostile Indians in north Florida, and settlers continued to die.

- March 30, 1838: Malachai Hogan, whose homestead was in the fork of the Ft. Crane and Ft. Tarver Roads, was killed and scalped, along with a companion, just outside the walls of Fort Micanopy.

- June 1838: A small skirmish was fought on Kanapaha Prairie, near Fort Walker. One soldier was killed and another six wounded.
- April 1839: Three settlers were killed while traveling along the edge of Paynes Prairie near Black Point, where the first shots of the Second Seminole War had been fired almost four years before.
- 1840: During a resurgence in hostilities around Paynes Prairie in 1840, a party of men were attacked as they made their way from Fort Wacahoota to Fort Micanopy. Killed were three men (including the teamster) and a couple of mules.
- 1840: Preacher McRae and another man were attacked about three miles from Micanopy. McRae was killed, and his companion got away, although he had been shot four times.
- May 19, 1840: One man was killed and three others escaped when they were attacked near Fort Micanopy by a band of eight to one hundred warriors led by Coacoochee. Seventeen soldiers under Lieutenant Sanderson pursued the hostiles and, in the battle that ensued, were badly beaten. Sanderson and five of his men were killed. As a gruesome final touch, the Indians cut off five of Sanderson's fingers and stuffed them into his mouth.
- May 24, 1840: At Fort Crum, on the west side of the Prairie, a number of planters seeking refuge had recently brought their families. Whatever sense of security they may have felt in the small stockade turned out to be false. It was besieged, and all were killed by Indians.
- 1840: Early in the year, Fort Clark also fell victim to the increased violence, and the structure was burned. No one is certain if it was done by Indians or by evacuat-ing settlers who found the water to be barely drinkable.
- December 28, 1840: The wife of Major Montgomery was being escorted from Micanopy to Fort Wacahoota, some ten miles away. As the party passed through a hammock

on the south side of Ledwith Lake, Mrs. Montgomery and her thirteen escorts were ambushed. Only one, Lieutenant Hopson, managed to escape back to Micanopy. Blame for the massacre was given to Halleck-Tustenuggee and a band of thirty renegades. This incident gained national attention, mainly because it involved a major's wife. After the massacre of Mrs. Montgomery's party, the Indians who had established large encampments near the Prairie began moving southward.

- One of the last skirmishes in the area occurred on August 31, 1841. On this occasion, ten soldiers were attacked as they made their way around the east rim of the Prairie, traveling from Fort Tarver to Micanopy. Three of them were killed. The region had been considered relatively safe for several months, so this latest incident surprised many people. In October, a large number of soldiers from nearby posts gathered at Fort Tarver. From there they made a thorough sweep of the entire area between Newnans Lake and the tiny settlement of Hogtown, looking for Indians.

Paynes Prairie was again becoming a safe place. For the soldiers at Fort Micanopy, boredom and the suffocating Florida heat made life unbearable. Fortunately, a cure for their mental state was close at hand. On August 5, 1841, Lieutenant Colonel Riley was sent by Colonel Worth to examine the troops at Micanopy and investigate reports that drunkenness was becoming a problem. What he found was more a saloon than an army post. In a letter to Colonel Worth, Riley said that the fort was in chaos, with the soldiers getting drunk every night, partying, and shooting their guns into the air. During his visit, ninety men were on sick report and another fifty to sixty were in the jail. Of the handful of men from each company who could make it to assembly, some were drunk and others were ravaged by hangovers. According to Riley, whiskey sellers outnumbered soldiers two to one. His recommendation to Worth was to shut the fort down.

The report seems to have had little effect, however, as seen in a dispatch sent on March 20, 1842, by Captain W. Seawell of the 7th infantry to his superiors at Cantonment Winfield Scott. In it he complained that some of the local settlers "consider it greatly to their interest to carry it [the whiskey trade] on; far more so than they consider the presence of troops necessary for the purpose of protecting against Indian depredations. . . . My first sergeant was killed by musician Hastings for taking from him 2 bottles of whiskey. . . ." Drunkenness had been a bad problem among the soldiers throughout the Florida campaign. As far back as 1837, Bemrose wrote at Fort Drane that even with disease and injuries, drunkenness was the army's most serious problem.

In 1842, with morale among the troops floundering and only about three to four hundred Indians left in the remote areas of the Everglades, continuation of the war seemed futile. On August 14 of that year, Col. William J. Worth declared the war over. It had been one of the costliest and bloodiest events in American history. In seven years, the Second Seminole War had cost fifteen hundred soldiers their lives in addition to the untold number of volunteers and civilians who were killed. The monetary toll was over $40 million.

For the Seminoles, the toll was more tragic. Besides the unknown number of dead, they also lost their homeland and their freedom. What they didn't lose was their determination to survive on their own terms. Hidden deep in the inaccessible reaches of the Everglades, the remaining Seminole population learned to live in their new environment. From that band of determined survivors came the several thousand Seminoles living throughout Florida today.

❦

11. *Civilization Comes to the Prairie*

❧

I n 1842, *Congress passed the Armed Occupation Act, which* provided a free homestead to anyone willing to settle in Florida. This and the absence of hostile Indians encouraged a new wave of immigrants, and by 1845, Florida's population was large enough to warrant statehood.

Cotton fields and orange groves were planted around Paynes Prairie, and land sales boomed. In 1849, much of the land that made up the Arredondo Grant was sold. Even the town of Micanopy was put on the block and sold to Joel Smith as part of a deal that included many acres south of the Prairie. Across the Prairie, oak forests that would one day give way to the University of Florida campus were bringing in seventy-five cents per acre. Land was even more of a bargain for railroad builders. This was due in large part to the efforts of David Levy Yulee, son of Micanopy pioneer Moses Levy and, by that time, a Florida senator. Yulee was the driving force behind passage of the Internal Improvement Act, which provided large land grants to railroad companies adjacent to any tracks they laid.

The first tracks into Alachua County belonged to the Florida Railroad Corporation. Yulee was its president. The railroad was actually just one leg of a steamboat-railroad system intended to move goods between the northeast coastal cities and those along the Gulf. It was felt that shipments brought by steamboat to northern Florida could be delivered quicker by rail across the state than if they had to continue by boat around the peninsula. The Florida Railroad was incorporated in 1853, and work on it was begun a short time later. The route would carry the trains between Fernandina and Cedar Keys, cutting across Alachua County from northeast to southwest. Micanopy and Newnansville were both about ten miles from the proposed track, meaning that any people or goods that required shipment by rail would have to endure a treacherous journey along miserable dirt roads to reach the station.

As soon as plans for the railroad began, the residents of Alachua County began making plans of their own. A meeting was held at Boulware Spring in 1853, at which the county's fate was decided. From all across the county, frontier folk made their way along paths and wagon roads to the picnic grounds near the north side of Paynes Prairie. There, they discussed whether or not to move the county seat from Newnansville to a location along the forthcoming railway. Local planters had already decided to build a town alongside the tracks; it was now just a matter of whether or not to make the proposed town Alachua County's seat. Persuasive arguments and an irresistible offer by local contractor Tillis Ingram to build a low-cost courthouse at the new site won the day.

The debate then turned to naming the new town. Two of the wealthier plantation owners in the area, Major Bailey and William Lewis, had different suggestions. Bailey, a patriot and war veteran, wanted the town named after the Seminole War hero Edmund P. Gaines. Lewis wanted it named after himself. After much debate (which almost turned into a brawl), the Bailey contingent won the day: the new town was to be called Gainesville. Lewis conceded defeat graciously, but the residents of Newnansville who had just lost the county seat did not. They nicknamed the new town "Hog Wallow." Unfortunately, this would not be the last blow Newnansville received from the railroad era. Some years later, another track would draw the remainder of Newnansville's dwindled population to a new town called Alachua, a couple of miles to the south. Newnansville, once the largest city in north central Florida, became a ghost town.

The vote to centralize the county seat was later repealed. In a second election, it was decided to divide the county, placing one courthouse in Micanopy and keeping one at Newnansville. The citizens of Newnansville were elated. But their joy ended when, in a third and final election, the decision to move the county seat to Gainesville was reinstated.

The first proposed site for Gainesville was Sugarfoot Prairie, but that location was later ruled out as unsuitable (an opinion that is probably not shared by the thousands of people now living in the area, near today's Butler Plaza). Then, in the third election, held in the fall of 1854, it was decided that Blackjack Ridge, several miles north of Paynes Prairie, would be the best location. The area was not only high and dry, but the sandy, blackjack oak forest for which it was named was much easier to clear than the live oak forests that covered most of the area. Land for the new town was obtained from Major Bailey, whose plantation sat near the headwaters of Sweetwater Branch. Another parcel obtained from the estate of Neamiah Brush brought the total to a little over 103 acres. Together, the parcels cost Alachua county taxpayers $642.51.

The settlers went right to work chopping down the blackjacks and replacing them with buildings. At about the same time, another crew was hard at work near Fernandina, clearing the way for the Florida Railroad. By the time the first passenger train came to Blackjack Ridge on April 21, 1859, the small, newborn community of Gainesville sat waiting for it in the forest clearing. There was, however, one minor problem. The townsfolk had miscalculated where the tracks would pass and had built the town center a half mile to the east.

Things looked very promising for the fledgling village. Cotton plantations were springing up all around the Prairie, and orange groves were slowly becoming more popular. Wild oranges, first introduced by the Spanish explorers, had become a delicacy to local Indians, especially the Seminoles, who liked to cut a hole in them and pour honey in or roast them over a fire. By the time of Gainesville's founding, orange trees were growing wild throughout the state.

Immigrants were more eager to move into the area now that the Indian wars had ended and the battered remnants of the Seminole population were secluded deep in the Everglades. But, in 1855, while the first wooden structures were being built in Gainesville, fighting broke out once again between the Seminoles and soldiers in south Florida. Suddenly, the residents of Alachua County were seeing Indians everywhere. The fact that there were only about four hundred Indians left in Florida, including women and children, didn't seem to comfort the locals. Nor did the fact that the few remaining Seminoles who were actually warriors were busy fighting in south Florida. Even after two local men were caught and jailed for making fake Indian tracks, the sightings continued in Alachua and surrounding counties.

Some residents fled to the larger towns, but most chose to stay to see what would happen. Then there was Bud Higgenbotham. He had apparently heard too many tales of the Indian wars, so he built a fort. So far, the "war" had not caused any local casualties or created any heroes for whom he could name the structure, so he settled on Fort Nancy, in honor of his patient and understanding wife. From his wooden stronghold near Boulware Spring, Bud waited anxiously for the Indians. They never came.

With the new rail connection to Fernandina, the outside world was now accessible to the citizens of Alachua County. Immigrants continued to pour into Gainesville, many from Georgia and South Carolina. By 1860, Gainesville's white population was 223. The number of blacks was considerable, especially on the outlying farms and plantations. On the Haile Plantation alone, there were nearly one hundred black slaves, living five to a cabin.

Alachua County now had a way to ship to and receive goods from the outside world more easily, but transportation

A remnant of the old Arredondo-Micanopy
stage road near Tacoma. *(Lars Andersen)*

around the countryside was still primitive. A stagecoach was established in 1860 that ran between Ocala and Gainesville by way of Micanopy. After leaving the Micanopy station, which sat on present-day Cholokka Boulevard, the coach would rumble out of town by way of Seminary Street, heading first to Arredondo, then on to Gainesville.

Mail was the usual cargo on the wooden coaches, but occasionally some brave soul who couldn't afford a private carriage would climb aboard. Anxious to make good time, the coachman would have to drive his four horses hard for them to pull the wooden wheels through the soft sand and mud. The route carried the coach, bumping and clattering, along the improved Indian trail between Levy Lake and Paynes Prairie. After skirting the southwest margin of the Prairie, closely paralleling the route of today's Wacahoota Road, the trail curved to the north.

In the twenty-first century, Micanopy still
retains its nineteenth-century charm. (Lars Andersen)

For a short distance, it followed present-day Williston Road (State Road 121) before veering off to the left. Two miles later, with the coachman blaring away on his bugle, the stage rolled into the tiny village of Arredondo. During a short stop, the driver would get whatever he needed to quench his thirst while his battered passenger tried to regain his land legs. At last, with four fresh horses, the coachman would boost his reluctant guest onto the rickety coach, and away they would go. After another stop at Gainesville, the stagecoach continued on to Newnansville, the end of the line. For nearly fifteen years, this same adventure was played out two or three times a week, depending on the condition of the coach and the coachman.

The Civil War Years
In early 1861, residents of Alachua were waiting eagerly for

the Florida Railroad to stretch the last few miles to Cedar Key. When the last rails were finally laid on March 1, 1861, the excitement was tempered by fears of impending war. Three days after the railroad opened, Abraham Lincoln was elected president. To the people of Florida, who had seceded from the union only two months earlier, this was bad news. On April 12, the Civil War broke out. Many young men from across the state, including many from Alachua County, were sent north to the various battlefronts.

Florida was looked upon to help feed the Confederate Army. Especially important were the vast herds of cattle that ranged across south Florida, primarily on the Caloosahatchee Prairies. These were mostly wild scrub cattle, remnants of the Spanish period, which made them difficult to handle. The forty days it took to drive the wild cattle from Caloosahatchee to Baldwin, where they were loaded on trains for shipment north, were full of hardships. One of the last stops for the herds before reaching Baldwin was Paynes Prairie, where they were fattened up after the long journey.

Besides having to chase off predators such as bears, wolves, and panthers, cattle drovers had to contend with Union raiders and Confederate deserters, who often lay in ambush. The hazards of the journey made the arrival of cattle sporadic at best. To remedy the situation, the Confederate leaders established the Cow Cavalry. Under the leadership of a cattle rancher named Jacob Summerlin, the Cow Cavalry was able to secure the three-hundred-mile supply route. Soon, a steady supply of nearly five hundred head of cattle per week began arriving at the Baldwin station, continuing until the end of the war.

In 1864, the war came to Florida. Federal leaders had grown concerned about the flow of supplies leaving Florida and made an effort to stop it. The main target was Lake City, but in an effort to keep this a secret, forays were made into other nearby areas. One of them was Gainesville. On February 15, 1864, Federal troops raided Gainesville, taking possession of the old Suwannee Hotel on the northwest corner of present-day University Avenue and Main Street. They made barricades of hay to block the four roads leading away from the intersection. At each roadblock, guards were posted, allowing people to enter the town but preventing anyone from leaving. The nearest Confederate troops were in Newnansville, completely unaware of the raid.

The attack may have gone unchallenged if it weren't for the bold action of a Confederate wife and her son who were visiting friends in town. Hoping to alert a nearby force of Rebel soldiers, the woman wrote a note describing Gainesville's plight and pinned it inside her son's coat. Then, following his mother's instructions, the boy approached the Yankee soldiers at the roadblock and convinced them to let him pass, saying he wanted to graze his horse in the fields north of town. Once out of sight, the boy rode to Newnansville and found Captain Chambers of the 2nd Florida Cavalry, to whom he delivered the news. Chambers, however, was less than eager to engage the enemy. According to L. Jackson and W. P. Settleworth, who rode with the Confederates, Chambers led his troops on a "very leisurely" ride back to Gainesville, "making many stops along the way."

At Gainesville, twelve to twenty-four men volunteered to follow Lt. Sam Reddick in a charge against the Yankee position. In the brief skirmish that followed, the entrenched Union soldiers, armed with sixteen repeater rifles, were able to hold their position and drive the Rebels back. One of Reddick's men was killed. That night the Union force withdrew from Gainesville, but their leaving was, according to Jackson and Settleworth, "anything but creditable to the officers in command of the Confederate forces." According to reports given by Union troops, the Yankees withdrew because they thought that the Rebels they had encountered were an advance unit of Florida's most feared commander, J. J. Dickison. They were wrong, but ironically it was Dickison's wife, visiting friends in Gainesville, who had written the secret note to the Confederates in Newnansville, and it was their young son who had bravely conned his way past the Union sentries to deliver it.

Later that same year, on August 17, another strike was made at Gainesville. On this occasion, nearly three hundred Yankee soldiers, commanded by Col. Andrew T. Harris, came through

Waldo, then skirted the eastern edge of Newnans Lake by way of Windsor. Turning west, they made their way toward Boulware Spring, where they were delighted to find an abandoned fort. It was Bud Higgenbotham's Fort Nancy. Leaving his supplies, plundered goods, and a small force of infantry at the fort to await the main force of foot soldiers, Colonel Harris rode into Gainesville with his cavalry. At Camp Lee, a military post that sat alongside Sweetwater Branch near the present-day Matheson Center, Harris' soldiers fought briefly with a company of thirty to forty home guards, most of whom were older men and young boys. It was an easy victory for the invaders.

Harris thought he had defeated the force under J. J. Dickison and, brimming with confidence, allowed his men to break ranks and plunder the town. In reality, Dickison was approaching Gainesville with a large force of seasoned fighters. Upon hearing of the approaching Confederates, Harris gathered his men at the railroad station, where he was determined to make a stand. Soon, Dickison's force arrived and for an hour and a half engaged in a punishing attack on the Yankee soldiers. Harris tried to lead an orderly retreat that got as far as the Beville Hotel. After making a desperate last stand, the Union soldiers were forced to scatter and flee the town in all directions. Nearly fifty-two Yankee soldiers were killed in the battle, and about three hundred were captured.

In the meantime, the bulk of the Union force, mostly black infantry, had arrived at the Boulware Spring encampment. Unaware of the battle taking place in Gainesville, they remained at camp. When they received news of the defeat, the soldiers quickly packed up and left along the same road on which they had arrived. On their way, they stopped at Colonel Lewis' plantation long enough to plunder four wagonloads of valuables and a handful of slaves. Dickison arrived at the plantation early the next morning and, after hearing the terrorized Mrs. Lewis tell what had happened, promised to retrieve all of her belongings. There are no accounts of what followed, but at ten o'clock that evening, Mrs. Lewis was amazed to see Dickison arrive with all of the stolen items except for one horse.

The Civil War ended eight months later, and Alachua County was able to resume its growth. Sea Island cotton was still grown extensively, but orange cultivation boomed. Neatly manicured orange groves were now replacing many of the old oak and pine forests that bordered the Prairie. The savanna itself was thick with cattle. In a very short time, Alachua County was back to its pre-war levels, when it led the rest of the state in livestock production.

❦

12. *Steamboats and Railroads*

❦

The Life and Death of Alachua Lake

In March 1867, the Prairie flooded, killing many cattle and sheep. Losses were heavy, but the flood surprised no one. Paynes Prairie's fickle nature was the stuff of legend dating back to the first prehistoric inhabitants. Everyone knew that sometimes the basin filled and before long the water dropped again. It had always been that way and would probably continue to be so forever.

No one was alarmed, therefore, when the waters began to rise again in 1871. But by 1873, when the water covered pastures and roads and engulfed homesteads, people became concerned. It was apparent that Alachua Sink had somehow been plugged, but no one knew how. There was much creative speculation about how it had happened. The theory with which everyone seemed to be most comfortable laid the blame on tourists and picnickers. A favorite amusement for visitors to the sink was to throw logs into the water and watch as they slowly spiraled toward the center and were then sucked under by the cavernous drain. It was assumed that some of the logs jammed and eventually stopped the water from draining.

When it became apparent that the lake was permanent,

plans were made by the local citizenry to drain it. A canal was proposed that would connect Prairie Creek to the River Styx. This would not only dry the lake by depriving it of its main water source, it would create a shipping connection between Newnans and Orange Lakes. The plans had to be abandoned when the Florida Legislature passed an act making Alachua Lake a navigable body of water, thereby protecting it. The residents around Paynes Prairie were forced to accept the fact that they now owned lakeside property. No longer able to grow crops in the fertile soil at the basin's edge, residents put their shovels and hoes into storage and brought out their fishing gear.

The new lake became something of a tourist attraction. Local entrepreneurs capitalized on this popularity. P. M. Oliver, a Gainesville hotel owner and outdoorsman who often acted as a guide for local hunting expeditions into the Gulf Hammock, built a park near Boulware Spring. Oliver dammed the runoff from the spring, creating a small lake for swimming, complete with a bathhouse and small leisure boat. A bowling alley, roller coaster, dance pavilion, boat-shaped swings, and a trap shoot were some of the other attractions at Oliver's Park.

A gathering at Oliver's Park. (Matheson Historical Center)

One of the biggest draws of the park—and eventually its downfall—was a zoo. It wasn't very large, featuring mostly birds, reptiles, and a variety of other small animals. The star attraction of the zoo was a large black bear, which was often kept chained to a tree near the park entrance. One day, in the fall of 1884, the bear broke free and attacked four boys who were alone in the park. Three of the boys managed to escape by diving into the lake, but the fourth, Willie Jeffries, was caught in a curtained dressing room on the dock and killed. When help arrived a few hours later, the bear too was killed. Oliver's Park was soon closed, and today all that remains is the name, which has been given to a small residential community nearby.

By far the greatest opportunities for local entrepreneurs were on the lake itself. Boats became a must for the residents around Alachua Lake, some of whom were even able to create an income for themselves by hauling produce and passengers. The rowboat freight barons of Alachua Lake were confronted with some major competition in 1883 when the Alachua Steam Navigation and Canal Company was established. Its fleet included a small steam yacht, the *Geo. W. Harris,* a small steamer

A steamboat that used to ply the waters of Paynes Prairie, drawn by James Calvert Smith. (Florida State Archives)

named the *Chacala,* and two barges. There was also a larger, sixty-six-foot steamer, but there's no record of its having been used on Alachua Lake. The company also dug a canal linking Alachua Lake to Lake Wauberg, where, according to Jess Davis, "quite a settlement of northern people" was located.

At several strategic places around the lake, landings were built to accommodate nearby residents. The primary landings on the south shore were Leitner's, located at Bolen Bluff, and another that was simply called the Ferry Landing, just northwest of Chacala Pond, close to where the observation tower now stands. Across the lake, Biven's Arm was an important port of call for the steamers. But by far the most important one was at Alachua Sink, where, after 1882, goods could be loaded directly onto trains of the Florida Southern Railroad, which connected Gainesville to Palatka.

The best-known steamer was the thirty-two-foot *Chacala.* Two captains, James Croxton and Edward Healey, operated it, alternating shifts. James Calvert Smith said that the boat had a recurring mechanical problem, which Captain Healey would remedy by

James Croxton piloted the little steamer Chacala *on Alachua Lake.*
(*Florida State Archives*)

For years, remains of this old steamer could be seen near Alachua Sink. (Matheson Historical Center)

adding weights to the engine valve and delivering a round of "proficient swearing," a technique that "improved the strength of the engine but not the passengers' comfort—especially the ladies."

For nearly ten years, the *Chacala* sputtered across the three- to five-foot-deep lake. In dry spells, the lake would drop a bit, making the voyage more interesting, if it could be made at all. So when the water level began to drop in 1891, the boat captains, although annoyed, were hopeful that the water would soon rise again. Near Biven's Arm, the *Chacala* sat mired in the muck. The water level in the lake continued to drop

*Cowboys looking across a field of dead fish left stranded
after Alachua Sink became unplugged.*
(Special Collections, P. K. Yonge Library, University of Florida)

slowly for over a year. Then, in 1892, a final gush of water into
the underground caverns dropped the water level at Alachua
Sink, which is deeper than the rest of the Prairie basin, eight
feet over a ten-day period. The receding water left fish high and
dry by the millions. After enjoying twenty years of good sport
fishing, local residents indulged in a final spree of fish gathering. Even the most pathetic fishermen, loaded down with all the
fish they could carry, stumbled home to astonished wives. But
the great Alachua Lake fish fry was short lived. As the dead fish
began to ripen and stink, people packed their gear and headed
home. Almost overnight, Alachua Lake had changed from a good
place to visit to a great place to avoid.

Paynes Prairie was back. In the years that followed, the abandoned wharves served as reminders of the once-magnificent lake,
and out in the grass-covered expanse of Biven's Arm, the *Chacala*
remained as a monument to the "steamboat era" in Alachua

County. Eventually, she decayed into the Prairie muck. All that remained was her propeller, which is now displayed at the Paynes Prairie State Preserve Interpretive Center, south of the Prairie.

Rails Around the Prairie

During the Civil War, some sections of the Florida Railroad's tracks were destroyed, and others became unusable for want of maintenance. Only the section between Gainesville and Baldwin was kept open to facilitate the shipment of supplies and cattle from Paynes Prairie to the war zone.

After the war ended, the company found it hard to recover and finally, in 1872, was forced to reorganize. The name was changed to the Atlantic, Gulf and West India Transit Company, but soon, after some additional reorganizing, this was mercifully shortened to the Florida Transit Railroad. By 1876, the company was back on its feet. In addition to the original line through Gainesville, tracks were laid along a new route that ran from Waldo to Hawthorne, then around the east side of Orange and Lochloosa Lakes to Ocala.

Another addition to the company's system was a short spur to Alachua Lake from Gainesville. It was this new rail access, combined with the increased use of steamboats on the lake, that brought an end to all remnants of the local stagecoach lines. The Transit, as it was fondly nicknamed, went through a dizzying number of reorganizations and name changes before being absorbed into the Seaboard Airline Company in 1902.

Another rail line was built to serve the growing needs of the Paynes Prairie region in 1881. The Gainesville, Ocala, and Charlotte Harbor Railroad was the company's name when it began clearing a narrow swath through the Florida wilderness, westward from Palatka. By the time the tracks reached Alachua Sink and Gainesville in 1882, the company's name had changed to the Florida Southern. The community of Perry (today's Rochelle), named for Madison Starke Perry, local plantation owner and fourth governor of the state, got a new boost from the passing tracks. So grateful were the residents that they

*Madison Starke Perry had a plantation on the site for-
merly occupied by Fort Crane. The community that grew
from this antebellum plantation was first called Perry
in his honor. It was later renamed Gruelle and
finally Rochelle. (Florida State Archives)*

renamed their town Gruelle after the railroad's chief engineer.

Micanopy residents were not nearly as impressed by the notion of being a "train town" as the Gruelle residents had been. A branch line was proposed that would run from Gruelle southward to Charlotte Harbor by way of Micanopy. But the thought of huge steam engines rumbling into town every day, whistles blaring, was more than the townsfolk could handle, so they refused access to the railroad. The railroad company was unfazed by the decision and simply bypassed the town several miles to the east. A small station was set up near the northwest corner of Orange Lake to serve the Micanopy area. To reach the station, called Micanopy Junction, Micanopy residents had to endure an arduous three-and-a-half-mile trek along a rugged road of soft sugar-sand and mud. Soon the locals were yearning to hear the sweet sound of train whistles in their town and weren't too proud to admit their change of heart. By the following year, jubilant townsfolk were gathered alongside a newly built spur from Micanopy Junction, as the first train rumbled into town, whistle blaring.

To further serve the fertile growing region south of Paynes Prairie, a short line was laid that ran north out of Micanopy. After passing to the east of Lake Wauberg, the tracks curved northwestward toward a small station called Ascot, near the present interpretive center at the state preserve. From there, the route headed across George's Pond and on to Tacoma. There was also a plan to put a trestle across the Prairie, but this project never materialized.

In 1895, the Gainesville and Gulf Railway Company laid tracks around the Prairie's western margin. Paynes Prairie was now completely encircled by railroad tracks. At short intervals along the G & G's route, stations were set up to serve nearby residents. Some of the stations, such as Tacoma, were located in established communities, while others, such as Clyatt's and Haile, were placed at strategic places along tracks and named for the families on whose property they sat. After closely following the route of the old stage road, the G & G trains would wind their way around the west side of the Prairie to Rocky Point. From there, a short ride brought them into Gainesville.

The stations along the G & G often became focal points around which small communities grew. In 1895, post offices were established at Tacoma, Kirkwood, Clyatt's, and Wacahoota Station at the extreme southwest corner of Paynes Prairie, but most went out of service by 1907 with the advent of rural delivery from Micanopy.

In 1906, the G & G was sold. The new owners made it a link in their proposed line to connect Tampa with Jacksonville. The Tampa and Jacksonville Railway Company, or T & J for short, operated for many years and became an integral part of life on the Prairie, although it never reached either Tampa or Jacksonville. In her book *The Story of Historic Micanopy,*

The T & J, nicknamed the "Tug & Jerk," crossing George's Pond near Tacoma. (Florida State Archives)

Caroline Watkins recalls the T & J letting out four sharp blasts on the whistle to warn everyone within earshot of impending bad weather. Until about 1930, travelers could get to Micanopy in passenger cars of the T & J trains but the ride was not much smoother than that of the stagecoaches of old. This inspired the nickname "Tug & Jerk." In 1943, demand for the train's service had fallen, forcing the T & J out of business. The rails were pulled up and sold to other railroad companies. Today, the overgrown roadbed can still be seen in some places along the north side of Wacahoota Road.

Yellow Fever

The railroads brought to the Prairie everything the outside world had to offer, which wasn't always good. In 1888, yellow fever rode the tracks into north central Florida, creating panic and leaving sixteen Gainesville residents dead in its wake. The epidemic began in Tampa early in the year and a short time later was reported in Jacksonville (early July) and Fernandina (early August). Gainesville residents were terrified that the disease would hit their town next. They had good reason to be afraid: ten years earlier, yellow fever had ravaged the Mississippi Delta region, killing nearly fifteen thousand people.

In Fernandina, the situation was complicated by striking longshoremen, who apparently were intent on stirring up trouble. The capabilities of the local law enforcement were not enough to handle the problem, so the governor of Florida ordered the Gainesville Guards to the small community just north of Jacksonville. The mayor of Gainesville suspected that there were already cases of yellow fever in Fernandina and protested to the governor. Fernandina's mayor repeatedly declared his town free of the disease, leaving the Gainesville Guards with no choice but to board the train bound for Fernandina. The boys must have been grateful to see the many townsfolk who had gathered at the station to see them off, but they probably could have done without the funereal tone of the sendoff, which included a slow dirge.

As everyone suspected, yellow fever was in Fernandina. The Guards completed their duty, came home, and on September 17, 1888, the first case of the disease was diagnosed in Gainesville. Armed guards were stationed at all train stops and roads that connected the community to the outside world. Called the "shotgun guards" because of their weapons, their mission was to prevent more carriers of the disease from coming into or leaving the town. People living around Paynes Prairie had to fend for themselves.

Yellow fever was still treated as a mystery when it hit in 1888, even though Dr. John Perry had discovered the disease's cause fifteen years earlier. Driven by the death of his wife and young daughter during an 1871 outbreak of yellow fever in Tampa, Dr. Perry successfully traced the disease's cause to the yellowhammer, or treetop, mosquito, but his findings went unnoticed. It wasn't until about 1900, almost thirty years after other researchers had confirmed Dr. Perry's findings, that the public and even the scientific community began to listen.

The residents of Alachua County in 1888 chose to rely on

archaic superstitions and unproven theories to try to combat the disease. Officials in Gainesville and the other infected cities fired cannons as prescribed by a theory that the concussion had an effect on the disease. Lime was dusted onto tree trunks, and a solution of bichloride of mercury was sprayed on the streets. Along major roadways, smudge fires of tar and pitch were burned, a standard procedure for dealing with any type of plague dating back hundreds of years. It would seem that in at least this one instance the attempt was probably effective, since mosquitoes, even those carrying disease, are driven off by smoke.

A quarantine camp for infected Gainesville residents was set up near the intersection of Williston Cutoff and Southeast Fourth Street, just west of Evergreen Cemetery. By the time the disease was gone, sixteen people had died, most of whom were buried in the camp. Many years later, when the Williston Cutoff was being prepared for pavement, the marked graves were moved to Evergreen Cemetery. A monument dedicated to the victims sat for many years on the lawn of the Alachua County Courthouse and in 1922 was moved to the main entrance of Evergreen Cemetery.

❦

13. *The Plunder of Paradise*

In the late 1800s, the nation was experiencing an incredible growth in industry, which brought with it a need for forest products of all sorts, primarily lumber. Oaks, magnolias, and many other species common to Southern woodlands were cut down and hauled away in great numbers. But the most valued trees were by far the pines.

Ecologically speaking, pinelands are much simpler forests than many others, containing fewer species. To most humans, pine trees are seen as a commodity, providing products such as lumber, paper, and turpentine. But there are those who see pines in a different light. In 1875, Sydney Lanier wrote that pines "signify the mystery of that repose that comes only from tested power and seasoned strength—a grandeur of tranquillity which is as much greater than the grandeur of cataclysms . . . as Lee's manhood is greater than Napoleon's." Apparently, besides being a huge fan of pine trees, Lanier was pretty fond of Robert E. Lee as well.

Others who had their eyes on the pines of post-Civil War Florida were looking more for profit than aesthetics, and the men doing the work were hardly poets. Dismal logging camps were scattered throughout the Florida backwoods. While hiking across Florida along the tracks of the Florida Railroad in 1867, the famous naturalist John Muir wrote about one such camp:"I came to a shanty where a party of loggers were getting out long pines for ship spars. They were the wildest of all the white savages I have met. The long-haired ex-guerrillas of the mountains of Tennessee and North Carolina are uncivilized fellows; but for downright barbarism these Florida loggers excel."

And it wasn't only for lumber that the pinelands were invaded. In other parts of north Florida's forest, crews were hard at work tapping the pine trees for turpentine. It was miserable work, and finding willing laborers was difficult until the convict lease system was established. After the Civil War, the arsenal at Chattahoochee was turned into an insane asylum/prison. Officials would often lease out strong prisoners to local turpentine operations, giving the companies plenty of leeway to deal with the convicts as they saw fit. With this lack of restraint, the companies developed some creative punishments for misbehaving convicts, the three most popular being hanging by the thumbs, confinement in a sweatbox without air or light, and "watering." In his book *The American Siberia,* Capt. J. C. Powell, a former boss over one such crew, describes watering

John Muir. *(Florida State Archives)*

as "no less than the celebrated torture practiced during the Spanish Inquisition under the name 'ordeal by water.'... The prisoner was strapped down, a funnel forced into his mouth and water poured in. The effect was to enormously distend the stomach, producing not only great agony but a sense of impending death, due to pressure on the heart. . . ."

Powell's squad did most of their turpentining north of Gainesville near Live Oak, but conditions were not much better for the men working the piney woods around Paynes Prairie. Usually, a system of peonage was established wherein the company that owned the turpentine operation had a company store for the workers. All supplies had to be bought at the store at high prices. By selling supplies to the workers on credit, the company prevented them from ever being able to save enough money to leave. With time, living conditions improved somewhat for the turpentiners, but the work was still very difficult. For many years Florida was a primary source of naval stores for the country. Even as late as 1941, the industry was still in full swing, with Florida

Turpentine still near Micanopy. (Florida State Archives)

supplying nearly twenty percent of the world's supply of turpentine and resin. It wasn't until after World War II that the introduction of petroleum-based solvents and synthetics began to replace turpentine, thus bringing an end to the industry.

Some of north Florida's hardwood species were also in demand during the late nineteenth century. Magnolias, a primary part of the naturally occurring hardwood forests around Paynes Prairie, were removed in large numbers and milled into slats for citrus shipping crates. Even the live oak, probably the area's most important tree species, came under attack. Centuries earlier, when the first European explorers saw live oak trees, they immediately appreciated the wood's unique qualities and great potential for shipbuilding. These men were all sailors familiar with the basics of boat making and knew good wood when they saw it. It was on the basis of one enthusiastic report about the abundance of live oaks that the Spanish rulers decided to attempt the first settlement in Florida at Pensacola Bay in 1559. The effort failed after only two years, four years before the more successful founding of St. Augustine.

From that time on, the strength and natural curves of live oak wood made it prized by shipbuilders worldwide. By the mid-1800s, demand became so great that elaborate scams were employed to poach live oak trees from the government lands where most of the forests were located. One ploy that was frequently used was for a Northern subcontractor to hire a poor Florida woodsman to build a cabin in a desired live oak hammock and claim squatter's rights. The subcontractor would then buy the trees from the squatter. In a matter of two to four weeks, the trees would be felled and the wood shipped off to some distant port. With the operation completed, the subcontractor rode away about $1,500 richer, and the squatter moved on, perhaps to set up house in another prospective oak hammock. All that remained of what had been a fine oak forest was a lot of stumps, some immature trees that had been spared the axe, and a small abandoned shack.

At first, most of this activity took place along the coast, where the wood could easily be shipped out, but with the arrival of rails, the inland regions became easily accessible and the trees around Paynes Prairie were logged out. Additional stress was put on local live oaks in land-clearing operations to make room for homesteads, orange groves, food crops, and pastures.

Spanish moss was another source of income for ambitious woodsmen of the late 1800s. Florida natives had used this interesting air plant for hundreds of years for clothing and medicine and as a binder for pottery. They also learned early on about the amazing tensile strength of the plant's wiry strands and would often use them to make twine and rope. When whites first encountered the plant, they found little use for it but marveled at its strange appearance. The early Spanish explorers, always happy to mock their French counterparts, called the plant *peluca francesca,* or "Frenchman's wig." Not to be outdone, the French referred to it as *barbe espanole*, or "Spanish beard," and it was from this that the name Spanish moss derived.

Carl Linnaeus, the eighteenth-century naturalist, was equally frivolous when he set about giving Spanish moss its scientific name, *Tillandsia usneoides.* "Tillands" was the nickname he had given one of his students, who became so seasick on a research voyage that he elected to travel two hundred miles by land to reach his home rather than take the much shorter boat ride. The name literally means "landlubber," which Linnaeus thought was appropriate for Spanish moss because of his mistaken theory that the tiny scales that cover the plant help keep out water. It would be many years before researchers realized that the scales actually help catch water.

The renewed interest in Spanish moss during the late nineteenth century was brought on by the furniture industry, which found that the plant's tough wiry core, when processed, made excellent stuffing. Moss gathering became the career of choice for many Alachua County woodsfolk who were not inclined to pursue conventional lifestyles. Moss pickers around Paynes Prairie could bring their harvest to one of several moss gins located in Gainesville, or they could make a little more money by curing it themselves. It was not uncommon to see the fence around a poor picker's shanty adorned with moss curing in the sun.

The Great Freeze

The greatest change to the landscape around Paynes Prairie in the late 1800s was the result of a whim of nature and not of man. A pair of hard freezes in the winter of 1894–1895 killed much of the local vegetation and completely wiped out the many citrus groves for which the region had become famous. Floridians had enjoyed oranges ever since Pedro Menéndez, the founder of St. Augustine, introduced them to the natives in 1565. The Indians loved them, and before long orange trees were growing near every native village in north Florida.

Both the Indians and Spaniards grew oranges for local consumption, so it wasn't until 1763, when England gained control of the state, that Northerners got their first taste of Florida oranges. When Florida came into American hands in 1821, immigrants were quick to establish commercial groves, especially along the St. Johns River, along which they could easily be shipped. Wild groves of sour oranges were already well established around Paynes Prairie by the time Americans began moving in and planting other varieties. But citrus cultivation was a minor industry until after the Civil War, when the new railroad access and improved varieties brought a boom. During the Alachua Lake period, no description of the area was complete without mention of vast groves and the heavy fragrance of orange blossoms on warm spring days.

In his book *Eden of the South,* Carl Webber opined that "... there is no doubt that the orange culture here in the 'Orange Belt' of Florida is one of the most substantial industries in the world." Webber was rightfully enthusiastic about the Alachua region and didn't mind saying so. "People from the north often ask if a frost may not sometime come and destroy the business of Orange culture. Certainly, it may, and so may the waters of the Atlantic Ocean sweep New England from the face of the earth." Such praise, mixed with a liberal dose of Southern pride, helped make Webber something of a local hero. Unfortunately, he was more gifted at delivering flamboyant accolades then at predicting the future.

In December 1894, a hard arctic blast dropped the temperature around Paynes Prairie to near 14°. The citrus trees were reduced to stumps. Within weeks, new shoots were growing from the stumps, and there was hope that in several years, with any luck, the orchards could recover. Luck, however, was in short supply, and two months later another freeze dealt the death blow to Paynes Prairie's citrus industry, with eleven-degree temperatures and a coating of snow. Commercial orange cultivation continued a short distance to the south, but around the Prairie the only oranges grown since then have been in private gardens. The empty fields where groves once stood were planted with vegetables or pine trees or were simply allowed to revert to natural forests.

❦

14. *Ditches, Dikes, and Highways*
✿

The Camp Ranch

In 1881, two years before the Chacala began the steamboat era on Alachua Lake, another important event took place in Alachua County that heralded one of the biggest economic booms in Florida's history. While digging on his property near Hawthorne, Dr. C. A. Simmons discovered calcium phosphate, a valuable substance for making fertilizer. He began mining the phosphate and processing it into fertilizer in 1883, but money was tight, and by the following year his operation was closed. His discovery didn't draw much attention, but soon other deposits began showing up around the state. By the early 1890s, Florida was a boom state. Land values soared, and many new towns were built near the larger mines.

One man who immigrated here to get a share of the wealth was a Virginia timber baron named William N. Camp. With his wife, Texie, Camp moved to a farm northwest of Gainesville and went to work establishing the Albion Mining and Manufacturing Company. By 1895, there were four hundred phosphate mining companies operating in central Florida, but the boom was beginning to subside. Many companies began to shut down. By the turn of the century, only about fifty were still operating, including Bill Camp's.

Camp was able to take advantage of lower land prices, buying some for as little as twenty-five cents per acre. By 1907, he was the largest landholder in Florida, with nearly 150,000 acres to his name. It was during this massive land-grabbing campaign that he bought Paynes Prairie, but it wasn't for phosphate. In his younger days, Camp had built a dam and power plant near Roanoke, Virginia. Using the skills acquired in Virginia and techniques he observed while visiting the Netherlands, Camp devised a unique power generator on the Withlacoochee River. Originally it was meant to serve only his nearby mining operation, but the system worked so well that his Florida Power Company was soon supplying power to much of the Withlacoochee area. It was his interest in generating power that prompted Bill Camp to buy Paynes Prairie. His intention was to plug Alachua Sink, recreating Alachua Lake, and then harness the lake's overflow to generate electricity. But he soon realized the project would be too costly and abandoned it.

Camp was still determined to make use of Paynes Prairie. Cattle owned by area ranchers grazed by the thousands on the marshy savanna. But Camp felt the Prairie was still not being used to its greatest potential. Its sogginess made much of the basin unusable, even for cattle. It was an unacceptable situation, which Camp was determined to fix. On November 12, 1911, he traveled to Gainesville and checked in at the Brown House. Townsfolk were curious why Bill Camp was there and soon learned that he had come to check on the progress of an army of surveyors who were busily laying the groundwork for his latest scheme. He was going to drain Paynes Prairie.

The prospect of having Paynes Prairie drained was welcome news in Gainesville. Harnessing and controlling nature was still seen as an undisputed sign of progress, with ideas like preservation and nature conservation still generations away. But excitement over the project came to an abrupt end when, two weeks after his Gainesville visit, Bill Camp died at his home in Ocala.

After Bill Camp's death, his son Jack continued to run the Paynes Prairie operation. At first, he rented the Prairie to the Lykes Brothers Company and other large cattle growers for four to five dollars per head per season. After being fattened up, the cattle were dipped in chemical vats to kill ticks and then shipped off to market. Eventually, Jack Camp began raising his own cattle. His herd of nearly thirty-five hundred cattle produced two thousand calves per year.

In addition to keeping the cattle ranch going, Jack Camp also kept alive his father's dream of draining the Prairie. In 1917, surveyors were again working on the Prairie. Although the Camps could not come up with a workable plan, by this time their dream had become infectious. In 1919, town leaders in Micanopy devised a plan to drain Tuscawilla Lake into Orange Lake by way of the River Styx. The lake, like Paynes Prairie, is at the mercy of a large sinkhole, or "suck hole," as the old timers used to call them. When the hole opens, the lake dries. Once, a cattleman who owned Tuscawilla Lake/Prairie tried to keep the hole from becoming clogged by building a wooden dam around it, which would keep debris out while letting water flow through. The plan backfired, however, when the barricade collapsed and plugged the cavern, causing the lake to fill to a remarkable level, with its eastern shore washing up to the embankment of Highway 441.

In Gainesville, the "dam-and-drain" fever had also taken hold. If the Camps couldn't do it, maybe the county could. On October 21, 1919, the *Gainesville Daily Sun* reported that a group of "progressive citizens of Gainesville" were proposing to drain Levy Lake, Paynes Prairie, and Orange Lake into the Oklawaha River, opening 150,000 acres of "undeveloped 'bad lands' " for development. It was speculated that the work would be done by Wills and Sons and McCarthy, a company that, by the time Florida's land reclamation frenzy ended years later, had carved a vast network of canals and dams throughout south Florida. Soon, however, proponents of the plan found other schemes to pursue, and the Prairie was given a temporary reprieve.

In 1926, heavy rains spawned a new round of discussions on how to control the Prairie. This time the focus was on the area from Lakes Santa Fe and Alto to Orange Lake. Paynes Prairie would be drained and Newnans Lake lowered about two feet. Unlike with previous discussions, there was a new sense of concern and urgency attached to the 1926 proposal. In short, a road, U.S. 441, was being built across the basin.

The residents of Micanopy were outraged by the idea, and in July the chamber of commerce passed a resolution to that effect. The proposal floundered, but by then the idea had gained momentum. Drainage of the Prairie seemed imminent. The flooding rains of 1926 had also concerned Jack Camp, but, unlike the county governments, he didn't have to please Micanopy or anyone else. The following year, he set twenty years of planning into motion.

By 1931, the work was near completion. A system of dikes and canals controlled water flow on the basin, while a dam and canal on the eastern edge diverted the inflowing water from Prairie Creek to the headwaters of the River Styx. From there, the water flowed to Orange Lake. By July, the Prairie's water level was dropping almost an inch a day. By fall, it was nearly dry.

The new system worked fairly well, but it wasn't foolproof, as the Camps discovered a decade later. In October 1941, Alachua County received twenty-one inches of rain in three days. The water level rose quickly in the basin, making it necessary to temporarily evacuate the cattle to drier parts of Florida and Georgia. But the canal did its job, and soon the Prairie dried.

Highways Across the Prairie

In 1923, most of the Micanopy Road (now the Wacahoota Road) and the section of Williston Road skirting the northwest edge of the Prairie were paved. That same year, construction began on the Highway 441 crossing of the basin. By 1926, Highway 441, dubbed the Dixie Highway, was paved from Lake City all the way to south Florida—except the two-mile stretch across Paynes Prairie. Travelers were forced to detour around the west side of the Prairie along the Wacahoota Road. It was a miserable trip. The road was paved only as far as Kirkwood, and even the paved section was deteriorating quickly because of the increased traffic load.

Part of the delay was due to a flood in 1925 that raised the Prairie's water level several feet. During the temporary flood, people were able to take small boats out onto the "lake" and reminisce about the bygone days of Alachua Lake. The north end of the Highway 441 road fill was used as a landing.

Finally, in the spring, the fill was opened to car traffic but was still unpaved. On May 20, the State Road Department announced it would be closing the fill for three days for paving. The sting of the announcement was soothed by assurances that "this is the last time the causeway will be closed, as it will then be completed." Two months later, the road was still unpaved, and traffic, averaging one and a half cars per minute, was having a devastating effect on the loose fill. Traffic was reduced to one lane, which would open for fifteen minutes for southbound traffic, then fifteen minutes for northbound. The entrances on the north and south sides were open for only five minutes, since it usually took nine to eleven minutes for a car to make the crossing.

By 1927, the road was complete. The steam shovel used by the L. M. Grey Company to dig the fill sat rusting for many years in the ditch alongside the highway near the south end. To some, it appeared the workers were so relieved to finally be done that they simply turned off the engine and walked away.

The next road on the Prairie came in the 1950s, when a two-mile fill was built, stretching westward from 441 near the middle of the basin to a newly built Federal Aviation Administration navigational facility. With most of the "active" water flow taking place on the east side of 441, this new dike did little additional harm to the Prairie's already suffering ecosystem.

The next and, to date, biggest structure built on Paynes Prairie was I-75. Completed in 1964, this highway allowed increasingly large numbers of people to spend increasingly short periods of time enjoying and destroying one of Florida's most important natural areas. The number of animals killed yearly on these two highways is staggering. In 1974, Richard Franz made a weekly count of snakes killed on the 441. From his observations, it was estimated that over eighteen thousand snakes died in one year on the road. Twenty years later, a study by the Department of Natural Resources found that nearly four times as many animals die on the two roads across Paynes Prairie than in any

As work began on Highway 441, the Prairie flooded. This view from Rocky Point shows the newly created "spit" of land, which was used as a temporary boat launch.
(Florida State Archives)

After dredging and filling the roadbed for Highway 441, this old dredge sat abandoned for many years alongside the road. (Matheson Historical Center)

*In the early days, northbound and southbound traffic took turns cross-
ing Highway 441 in 15-minute shifts. The highway would open
for 5 minutes on one side of the Prairie. After those cars made
the 10-minute drive across, cars on the opposite side
would be allowed to cross.*
(Matheson Historical Center)

other park in the state. The fatalities listed in the 1993 study
included seven deer, four gray foxes, and three bobcats.

For travelers on I-75 who want a good view of the savanna, the southbound rest area on the Prairie's north rim is one
of the best. It was recently made even better with the construction of an observation platform built in the shape of a
huge snake. Unfortunately, the northbound rest area across the
highway is more surrounded by trees. Travelers stopping there
to rest have to content themselves with viewing each other or
their southbound comrades, strolling serenely along the observation deck across the highway.

✻

15. *Paynes Prairie State Preserve*
❧

Paynes Prairie became a state preserve in 1970. With the scratch of a pen and the exchange of $5.1 million, a 17,346-acre tract of the basin and surrounding uplands became the property of the state. Most of it was bought from Camp Ranch Incorporated, which agreed to allow the exchange of money and land to be spread out over three years. Without this arrangement, the state could not have made the deal. This gradual exchange also gave Camp Ranch plenty of time to wind down its huge operation and relocate its cattle.

The series of events that led up to the 1970 purchase started thirteen years earlier with a pet project of the Gainesville Garden Club. Headed by the late Marjorie Carr, wife of famous biologist and sea turtle researcher Archie Carr, the Garden Club began efforts in 1957 to educate the public about the Prairie's importance and to get it protected. On March 21, 1961, their hard work and devotion were rewarded when Paynes Prairie was given the status of an official wildlife sanctuary—the first in Florida.

The title "wildlife sanctuary" looked good on paper, but it soon became clear that the Prairie was still not safe from the whims of civilization. Apparently, the term "sanctuary" was flexible, and soon a handful of ideas surfaced as to which animals should be protected, in what manner, and for what purpose. One of the first proposals to be presented formally—and the one that would endure the longest—was Howard Bishop's suggestion to flood the Prairie and resurrect the long-dead Alachua Lake. The plan called for buying the Prairie and some surrounding high ground, building campsites and recreational facilities, raising Highway 441 a few feet, and then flooding the basin. After so many decades of unchallenged, even praised, efforts to drain the Prairie, it's hard to imagine Bishop's proposal getting local support. But it did. Thoughts of a quiet, safe haven for wild animals quickly gave way to dreams of bolstered tourism, good fishing, and enhanced land values. Support from organizations such as the Gainesville Motel Association, Alachua County Sportsman's Association, and Gainesville Boat Club was to be expected, but many were surprised to learn that the Alachua County Audubon Society and even the Gainesville Garden Club also were endorsing the idea.

After the initial flush of enthusiasm, the proposal to reflood Paynes Prairie lost momentum. The biggest obstacle was the county commission's refusal to allocate money for a feasibility study. But there was one commissioner who refused to abandon hope. Edgar Johnson took up the call to flood with a passion and continued to work behind the scenes, meeting with state and federal officials for years after the matter was all but forgotten by everyone else.

The debate was finally put to rest with Florida's 1970 purchase of the Prairie. Now it was the state's turn face the challenge of what to do with the Prairie. Flooding was not an option—there were still privately owned sections of the basin, and there was Highway 441. The state's intention was to preserve the tract in its natural state, so the only questions remaining were what its natural state was and whether it could be recreated. Should they just leave the area alone and let it fend for itself, or should they try to revive an earlier, less-altered version?

After some deliberation, it was decided to restore the Prairie as William Bartram had described it in 1774 or, more accurately, to restore it as much as possible. Some of the species from

Bartram's time had become extinct, including the Carolina parakeet, the ivory-billed woodpecker, and the migratory passenger pigeon. Others, such as the Florida panther and the red wolf, are now gone from this area but survive elsewhere.

There have also been some newcomers to the local animal population in the past two hundred years. When several house sparrows were released in New York's Central Park in 1850, no one imagined that within fifty years they would range across much of North America, including north Florida. Nor did anyone think that a hundred starlings released in that same park in 1890 would spread with equal speed. But they did, and today these two exotic species are common on Paynes Prairie as well as in the rest of the state. And Bartram's imaginative writing style would probably have been stretched to the limit if he had encountered the nine-banded armadillo. This interesting mammal has been residing in the Florida wilds only since escaping captivity in Miami in the 1920s.

One step toward restoring the Prairie's early fauna came in 1975 with the release of ten bison. These large grazers were residents of Florida for many thousands of years before humans arrived but never in huge herds like out West. (Florida's thick tangle of forest growth is not well-suited to large herds of animals. Even the earliest records describe a meager population. Bartram saw none.) The bison adapted well to their new habitat and by the mid-1980s numbered thirty-five. But then tragedy struck. Some nearby cattle contracted a highly contagious bovine disease known as *Brucellosis,* and before long the disease spread to the Paynes Prairie bison. The disease is not always fatal to bison but causes problems with reproduction and is highly contagious to many other species. So, one by one, as the animals became infected, they had to be slaughtered. By the time the disease had run its course, the ravaged herd was composed of just three females. The donation of one bull brought the total to four animals. From this meager stock, Paynes Prairie's bison population is again growing and, as of this writing, is up to twelve animals.

The Spanish horse is another animal that was reintroduced to Paynes Prairie. In 1985, one stallion and six mares were donated to the Preserve. Later, another stallion was acquired, and from this stock the herd has grown. This breed arrived in the New World with the first Spanish conquistadors and would later become an important part of daily life during every major period that followed. They were used by the Spaniards at La Chua Ranch, they were the famous Seminole horses of the eighteenth and nineteenth centuries, and they were the Cracker horses that helped tame the Florida frontier.

The flora on and around Paynes Prairie is also being restored. The heavy demands put on the forest in the past century are still apparent, and there are not many trees in the surrounding forests that are more than one hundred years old. But the cutting has stopped, and in some areas the once-common longleaf pine forests are being revived. Another difference from the past is the species distribution on present-day Paynes Prairie. Some of the native species, such as Southern magnolia, are much more scarce than they would be normally, while stands of water oaks and laurel oaks are more prevalent because of the lack of forest fires. A number of introduced exotic species are also flourishing. Some plants, such as certain varieties of grass that were introduced by cattlemen and Chinese tallow trees that escaped from the yards of local homeowners, are enjoying life here and are not likely to be eradicated.

Man's past attempts to civilize and control Paynes Prairie and the surrounding area have left the landscape scarred by a maze of dikes and canals. In an effort to make the best of this unfortunate reality, the park service has modified some of these unnatural features for use by visitors and park personnel. One of the earliest plans was to build a tram for tourists across the Prairie. This idea was shuffled around for a good part of the mid-1970s but was eventually dropped. Other projects have had more success.

In 1989, the Florida Department of Natural Resources bought a section of the abandoned railroad bed of the Atlantic Coastline Railroad, between Boulware Springs and Hawthorne. It was then converted into a trail for hikers, bicyclists, and horseback riders with several overlook platforms along the way for viewing the Prairie. Opened in January 1992, the Gainesville-Hawthorne State Rail Trail quickly became a popular way to explore the upland habitats and terrain along the Prairie's northeast rim. In 1996, concern for some of the local wildlife prompted state officials to reroute a section of the trail away from the Prairie's edge. The new section was opened in 1997. Overlooks that are bypassed by the new route can still be accessed by spur trails.

Out on the basin itself, rangers use old dikes built by Camp Ranch in their efforts to maintain and restore the Preserve. Some of the dikes have been made into trails that allow visitors to hike into the heart of the Prairie. On the La Chua and Bolen Bluff Trails, raised observation platforms allow you to get above the nearby vegetation and take in the view. But the best view is at the forty-eight-foot observation tower near the main visitor's center. Opened in 1981, the visitor's center is housed in a nice, large building on the Prairie's south edge. Inside is an auditorium for viewing videos about this and other state parks, as well as displays of artifacts and pictures telling about the Prairie's past and describing the plants and animals found there today.

To date, William Bartram's vision of Paynes Prairie's becoming "one of the most populous and delightful seats on earth," accommodating "in the happiest manner above one hundred thousand human inhabitants, besides millions of domestic animals," has not become a reality. We can only hope that his wide range of talents did not include foretelling the future and that Paynes Prairie will remain a sanctuary for old Florida's flora and fauna.

Some day, with luck and a lot of diplomacy and planning, there may come a time when the old dikes and Camp's canal can be eliminated. But restoring the area to its natural state is easier said than done. With two major highways crossing the basin and a number of privately owned tracts in the surrounding low areas, it would be disastrous simply to level all of the dikes and fill Camp's canal. The needs of the people living around Orange Lake, who have been receiving extra water through Camp's canal since the 1930s, would also have to be considered. But Orange Lake and Paynes Prairie were both thriving long before

Aerial view of Alachua Sink (lower left) and Alachua Lake (top center). One of the old dikes (highlighted by La Chua Trail, which runs on top of it) and the adjacent canal connecting the two bodies of water are reminders of the misguided efforts to control Paynes Prairie's fluctuating water levels. (Lars Andersen)

the canal was built. Any reference to the natural condition of these places must refer to the time before dredges arrived. There is nothing natural about Camp's canal.

Change has been the hallmark of Paynes Prairie's existence ever since the first sinkhole appeared that would one day spread into the huge basin we know today. Usually change comes at a much slower rate than that which humans have brought to the Prairie in the past few hundred years, but as long as it is protected from the ravages of man, nature will take care of itself. No matter what happens, the ecosystems of Paynes Prairie and the surrounding forests will never again be exactly as Bartram saw them. With a new selection of plant and animal species, the ecosystems around and on Paynes Prairie will be unique, different not only from all other ecosystems of the world, but from those in its own past as well.

❦

Bibliography

Albornoz, Miguel. *Hernando De Soto: Knight of the
    Americas.* New York: Franklin Watts, 1986.
"A Physician's Second." *National Intelligencer* (November 1,
    1943).
Arnade, Charles W. *Cattle Raising in Spanish Florida.* St.
    Augustine, Florida: St. Augustine Historical Society,
    1965.
Bacon, Eve. *Orlando: A Centennial History.* Chuluota,
    Florida: Mickler House Publishers, 1975.
Balseiro, Jose Agustin, ed. *The Hispanic Presence in Florida.*
    Miami: E. A. Seeman Publishing, Inc., 1976.
Bartram, William. *Travels through North and South
    Carolina, Georgia, East and West Florida, the
    Cherokee Country, the Extensive Territories of the
    Muscogulges, or Creek Confederacy, and the
    Country of the Chactaws.* Edited by Van Dorn. New
    York: Dover Publications, 1928.

Bemrose, John. *Reminiscences of the Second Seminole War.* Gainesville: University of Florida Press, 1966.

Blakey, Arch Frederic. *The Florida Phosphate Industry.* Cambridge, Massachusetts: Harvard University Press, 1973.

Boyd, Mark F., Hale G. Smith, and John W. Griffin. *Here They Once Stood.* Gainesville, Florida: University of Florida Press, 1951.

Brady, Tom. *The Story of Fort Micanopy.* Micanopy, Florida: Tom Brady Designs, 1990.

Brown, Robin C. *Florida's First People.* Sarasota, Florida: Pineapple Press, Inc., 1994.

———. *Florida's Fossils.* Sarasota, Florida: Pineapple Press, Inc., 1988.

Bucholz, F. W. *History of Alachua County Florida.* St. Augustine, Florida: The Record Co. Printers, 1929.

Burnett, Gene M. *Florida's Past: People and Events that Shaped the State.* 3 vols. Sarasota, Florida: Pineapple Press, Inc., 1986, 1988, 1991.

Bushnell, Amy. *The King's Coffer.* Gainesville: University Presses of Florida, 1981.

Campbell, Richard L. *Historical Sketches of Colonial Florida* (facsimile reproduction of 1892 edition). Gainesville: University Presses of Florida, 1975.

Chaffee, H. J. "Florida Forts Established Prior to 1860" (typescript). P. K. Young Library of Florida History, University of Florida, Gainesville, 19—(?).

Clausen, Carl J. "The A-356 Site in the Florida Archaic" (unpublished master's thesis). Department of Anthropology, University of Florida, Gainesville, 1964.

Corkran, David H. *The Creek Frontier: 1540-1783.* Norman: University of Oklahoma Press, 1967.

Covington, James W. "Migration of the Seminoles into Florida." *Florida Historical Quarterly,* vol. XLVI, no. 4 (April 1977): 340-357.

Cox, Merlin G., and J. E. Dovell. *Florida from Secession to Space Age.* St. Petersburg, Florida: Great Outdoors Publishing Co., 1974.

Cumbaa, Stephen. "An Intensive Harvest Economy in North Central Florida" (typescript master's thesis). University of Florida, Gainesville, 1972.

Davis, Jess G. *History of Alachua County.* Gainesville, Florida: Alachua County Historical Commission, 1959.

Derr, Mark. *Some Kind of Paradise.* New York: William Morrow and Co., Inc., 1989.

Douglas, Marjory Stoneman. *Florida: The Long Frontier.* New York: Harper and Row, 1967.

Evitts, William J. *Captive Bodies, Free Spirits.* New York: Julian Messner Publishing, 1985.

Fernald, Edward A., ed. *Atlas of Florida.* Tallahassee: Florida State University Foundation, Inc., 1981.

Forbes, James Grant. *Sketches of the Floridas* (facsimile reproduction of 1821 edition). Gainesville: University of Florida Press, 1964.

Francke, Arthur E., Jr. *Fort Mellon: 1837-42.* Miami, Florida: Banyan Books, Inc., 1977.

Fribleman, Peter. *The Bayous.* Alexandria, Virginia: Time-Life Books, Inc., 1973.

Fritz, Florence. *Unknown Florida.* Coral Gables, Florida: University of Miami Press, 1963.

Gainesville Sun (Gainesville Daily Sun), various issues, 1890-present.

Garrison, Webb. *A Treasury of Florida Tales.* Nashville, Tennessee: Rutledge Hill Press, 1989.

Gentleman of Elvas. *The Narratives of Desoto.* Translated by Buckingham Smith. Gainesville, Florida: Kallman Publishing Co., 1968.

Giddings, Joshua. *The Exiles of Florida* (facsimile reproduction of 1858 edition). Gainesville: University of Florida Press, 1964.

Gill, Joan E., and Beth R. Read. *Born of the Sun.* Hollywood, Florida: Florida Bicentennial Commemorative Journal, Inc., 1975.

Grismer, Karl H. *Tampa.* St. Petersburg, Florida: St. Petersburg Printing Co., 1950.

Hann, John H. *Apalachee: The Land between the Rivers.* Gainesville: University Presses of Florida, 1988.

Henderson, Ann, and Gary Mormino, eds. *Spanish Pathways in Florida.* Sarasota, Florida: Pineapple Press, Inc., 1991.

Hildreth, Charles Halsey. *A History of Gainesville.* Gainesville: University of Florida Press, 1954.

Jahoda, Gloria. *Florida: A Bicentennial History.* New York: W. W. Norton, Inc., 1976.

Johns, John E. *Florida During the Civil War.* Gainesville: University of Florida Press, 1963.

Jones, Kenneth M. *War with the Seminoles.* New York: Franklin Watts, Inc., 1975.

Josephy, Alvin M., Jr. *The Indian Heritage of America.* New York: Alfred A. Knopf, 1968.

Kearney, Bob, ed. *Mostly Sunny Days.* Miami, Florida: The Miami Herald Publishing Co., 1986.

Keel, James R. *Florida Trails to History's Treasure.* Ft. Lauderdale, Florida: Seajay Enterprises, Inc., 1981.

Kennedy, Stetson. *Palmetto Country.* Tallahassee: Florida A & M University Press, 1942.

Lanier, Sidney. *Florida: Its Scenery, Climate and History* (facsimile reproduction of 1875 edition). Gainesville: University of Florida Press, 1973.

Laudonnière, René. *Three Voyages.* Translated by Charles E. Bennett. Gainesville: University Presses of Florida, 1975.

Laumer, Frank. *Massacre.* Gainesville: University of Florida Press, 1968.

Lauter, Fred. "Steam-Boating in Alachua County, 1870–1905" (typescript). Gainesville Public Library, Gainesville, Florida, 1950.

Le Moyne, Jacques. *Narrative of Le Moyne.* Translated by Fred B. Perkins. Boston: Osgood Co., 1875.

Lyon, Eugene. *The Enterprise of Florida.* Gainesville: University Presses of Florida, 1976.

Mahon, John K. *History of the Second Seminole War.* Gainesville: University of Florida Press, 1953.

Martin, Richard A. *Eternal Spring.* St. Petersburg, Florida: Great Outdoors Publishing Co., 1966.

Martin, Sidney Walter. *Florida During the Territorial Days.* Philadelphia: Porcupine Press, 1974.

Martindell, David J. *The Florida Book of Trivia, Trifles, Facts and Firsts.* Islamorada, Florida: Tropical Attractions, Inc., 1983.

Maynard, Theodore. *Desoto and the Conquistadores.* New York: Longmans, Green and Co., 1930.

McCall, Maj. Gen. George. *Letters from the Frontier* (facsimile reproduction of 1868 edition). Gainesville: University Presses of Florida, 1974.

McDonald, Ida. "Paynes Prairie" (typescript). P. K. Young Library of Florida History, University of Florida, Gainesville, 1934.

McReynolds, Edwin C. *The Seminoles.* Norman: University of Oklahoma Press, 1957.

Milanich, J., and C. Fairbanks. *Florida Archaeology.* New York: Academic Press, 1980.

Milanich, J., and Charles Hudson. *Hernando de Soto and the Indians of Florida.* Gainesville: University Press of Florida, 1993.

Milanich, J., and Samuel Proctor. *Tacachale.* Gainesville: University of Florida Press, 1978.

Milanich, Jerald T. "Excavations at the Richardson Site." Bureau of Historical Sites and Properties, bulletin #2 (1972): 35-61.

———. "Two Cades Pond Sites in North Central Florida." *Florida Anthropologist,* vol. 31: 151-173.

Muir, John. *A Thousand-Mile Walk to the Gulf.* Boston: Houghton-Mifflin Co., 1916.

Mullins, Sue Ann. "Archaeological Survey and Excavation in the Paynes Prairie State Preserve" (master's thesis). University of Florida, 1977.

Myers, Ronald L., and John J. Ewel, eds. *Ecosystems of Florida.* Orlando: University of Central Florida Press, 1990.

Norman, Parke. *Exploding the Myths about Fabulous Florida.* Moore Haven, Florida: Rainbow Books, 1983.

Ott, Eloise, and Louis Chazal. *Ocali Country.* Ocala, Florida: Marion Publishers, 1966.

Patrick, Robert W. *Florida Fiasco.* Athens: University of Georgia Press, 1954.

Peters, Virginia Bergman. *The Florida Wars.* Hamden, Connecticut: Archon Books, 1979.

Pickard, John B. *Florida's Eden.* Gainesville, Florida: Maupin House, 1994.

Porter, Charlotte M. "William Bartram's Travels in the Indian Nations." *Florida Historical Quarterly,* vol. 70 (1992): 434-450.

Powell, J. C. *The American Siberia* (facsimile reproduction of 1891 edition). Gainesville: University Presses of Florida, 1976.

Quigg, Joyce A. "Paynes Prairie" (typescript). P. K. Young Library of Florida History, University of Florida, Gainesville, 1958.

Reese, M. Lisle. *Bean Soup.* Jacksonville, Florida: Crawford Publishers, 1964.

Roberts, William. *An Account of the First Discovery and Natural History of Florida* (facsimile reproduction of 1763 edition). Gainesville: University Presses of Florida, 1976.

Rouse, Parke, Jr. *The Timber Tycoons: The Camp Families of Virginia and Florida.* Richmond, Virginia: The William Byrd Press, 1988.

Schell, Rolfe F. *History of Fort Myers Beach, Florida.* Fort Myers Beach, Florida: Island Press, 1980.

Seaberg, Lillian M. "The Zetrouer Site" (master's thesis). University of Florida, 1955.

Sears, William H. "Melton Mound #3." *Florida Anthropologist,* vol. 9 (December 1956): 87-100.

Simmons, William H. *Notices of East Florida* (facsimile reproduction of 1822 edition). Gainesville: University of Florida Press, 1973.

Skinner, W. B., and Dr. W. George Gaines. *Adventurers in Florida History.* Pensacola, Florida: Town & Country Books, 1974.

Smith, James Calvert. "Micanopy" (typescript). Gainesville Public Library, 1942.

Smith, Lyman B. *The Bromeliads.* Cranbury, New Jersey: A. S. Barnes and Co., Inc., 1969.

Swanton, John R. *The Indians of the Southeastern U.S.* Washington, D.C.: Smithsonian Institution Press, 1946, 1987.

Tebeau, Charlton W. *A History of Florida.* Coral Gables, Florida: University of Miami Press, 1971.

Vanderhill, Burke G. "The Alachua Trail: A Reconstruction." *Florida Historical Quarterly,* vol. LV, no. 4 (April 1977): 423-437.

Vega, Garilasco de La. *The Florida of the Incas.* Translated by John and Jeanette Varner. Austin: University of Texas Press, 1951.

Walton, George. *Fearless and Free.* Indianapolis: Bobbs-Merrill, 1977.

Watkins, Caroline B. *The Story of Historic Micanopy.* Gainesville, Florida: Alachua County Historical Commission, 1976.

Watts, W. A. "Post Glacial and Interglacial Vegetation History of Southern Georgia and Central Florida." *Ecology,* vol. 52 (1971): 676–689.

Weddle, Robert S. *Spanish Seas.* College Station: Texas A & M University, 1985.

Weisman, Brent Richards. *Like Beads on a String.* Tuscaloosa: University of Alabama Press, 1989.

Williams, John Lee. *The Territory of Florida* (facsimile reproduction of 1837 edition). Gainesville: University of Florida Press, 1962.

Wood, Virginia Steele. *Live Oaking.* Boston: Northeastern University Press, 1981.

Wright, J. Leitch, Jr. *Creeks and Seminoles.* Lincoln: University of Nebraska Press, 1986.

Index

If you enjoyed reading this book, here are some other books from Pineapple Press on related topics. For a complete catalog, write to Pineapple Press, P.O. Box 3899, Sarasota, FL 34230 or call 1-800-PINEAPL (746-3275). Or visit our website at www.pineapplepress.com.

Best Backroads of Florida by Douglas Waitley. For vacationers and residents who want to catch a glimpse of the Florida of yesteryear, this book offers ten single-day backroads tours in the central part of the state on little-traveled byways. Get out of the car to enjoy beautiful picnic areas, lake and river cruises, airboat rides, snorkeling and scuba diving, and biking and hiking through the beauty of Florida's heartland. ISBN 1-56164-189-8 (pb)

Exploring Wild Central Florida by Susan D. Jewell. One of a series of field guides, each with information on all the parks, preserves, and natural areas in its region, including wildlife to look for and best time of year to visit. This one takes you from New Smyrna and Crystal River in the north to Hobe Sound and Punta Gorda in the south, including Lake Okeechobee. ISBN 1-56164-082-4 (pb)

The Florida Chronicles by Stuart B. McIver. A series offering true-life sagas of the notable and notorious characters throughout history who have given Florida its distinctive flavor. **Volume 1**: *Dreamers, Schemers and Scalawags* ISBN 1-56164-155-3 (pb); **Volume 2**: *Murder in the Tropics* ISBN 1-56164-079-4 (hb); **Volume 3**: *Touched by the Sun* ISBN 1-56164-206-1 (hb)

The Florida Keys by John Viele. The trials and successes of the Keys pioneers are brought to life in this series, which recounts tales of early pioneer life and life at sea. **Volume 1**: *A History of the Pioneers* ISBN 1-56164-101-4 (hb); **Volume 2**: *True Stories of the Perilous Straits* ISBN 1-56164-179-0 (hb); **Volume 3**: *The Wreckers* ISBN 1-56164-219-3 (hb)

Florida Portrait by Jerrell Shofner. Packed with hundreds of photos, this word-and-picture album traces the history of Florida from the Paleo-Indians to the rampant growth of the late twentieth century. ISBN 1-56164-121-9 (pb)

Florida's Past Volumes 1, 2, and 3 by Gene Burnett. Collected essays from Burnett's "Florida's Past" columns in *Florida Trend* magazine, plus some original writings not found elsewhere. Burnett's easygoing style and his sometimes surprising choice of topics make history good reading. **Volume 1** ISBN 1-56164-115-4 (pb); **Volume 2** ISBN 1-56164-139-1 (pb); **Volume 3** ISBN 1-56164-117-0 (pb)

Guide to the Lake Okeechobee Area by Bill and Carol Gregware. The first comprehensive guidebook to this area of the state includes a 110-mile hike/bike tour on top of the Herbert Hoover Dike encircling the lake, part of the Florida National Scenic Trail. ISBN 1-56164-129-4 (pb)

Guide to the University of Florida and Gainesville by Kevin M. McCarthy and Murray Laurie. Each significant building on campus and in town is described here, with information on its history, architecture, and current use. Fifteen maps and over 100 black-and-white photographs complete this thorough tour. ISBN 1-56164-134-0 (pb)

The Gulf of Mexico by Robert H. Gore. A synopsis of the history, geology, geography, oceanography, biology, ecology, and economics of this great body of water. The only book of its kind. ISBN 1-56164-010-7 (hb)

Key Biscayne by Joan Gill Blank. This engaging history of the southernmost barrier island in the U.S. tells the stories of its owners and would-be owners. ISBN 1-56164-096-4 (hb); 1-56164-103-0 (pb)

Poisonous Plants and Animals of Florida and the Caribbean by David W. Nellis. An illustrated guide to the characteristics, symptoms, and treatments for more than 300 species of poisonous plants and toxic animals. ISBN 1-56164-111-1 (hb); 1-56164-113-8 (pb)

Southeast Florida Pioneers by William McGoun. Meet the pioneers of the Palm Beach area, the Treasure Coast, and Lake Okeechobee in this collection of well-told, fact-filled stories from the 1690s to the 1990s. ISBN 1-56164-157-X (hb)

The Springs of Florida by Doug Stamm. Take a guided tour of Florida's fascinating springs in this beautiful book featuring detailed descriptions, maps, and rare underwater photography. Learn how to enjoy these natural wonders while swimming, diving, canoeing, and tubing. ISBN 1-56164-054-9 (hb); 1-56164-048-4 (pb)